COMMUNITIES OF DISSENT

COMMUNITIES OF DISSENT

A History of Alternative Religions in America

STEPHEN J. STEIN

OXFORD
UNIVERSITY PRESS

OXFORD
UNIVERSITY PRESS

Oxford University Press

Oxford New York
Auckland Bangkok Buenos Aires Cape Town Chennai
Dar es Salaam Delhi Hong Kong Istanbul Karachi Kolkata
Kuala Lumpur Madrid Melbourne Mexico City Mumbai Nairobi
São Paulo Shanghai Singapore Taipei Tokyo Toronto

Published by Oxford University Press, Inc.
198 Madison Avenue, New York, New York 10016
www.oup.com

Oxford is a registered trademark of Oxford University Press

Library of Congress Cataloging-in-Publication Data

Stein, Stephen J.,
Communities of dissent : a history of alternative religions in America/
Stephen J. Stein.
    p. cm.
Includes bibliographical references and index.
    ISBN 0-19-515825-3 (alk. paper)
    1. Cults—United States—History. 2. Sects—United States—History.
    3. United States—Religion. I. Title.
    BL2525 .S74 2002
    291.9'0973—dc21
                        2002006219

9 8 7 6 5 4 3 2 1

Printed in the United States of America
on acid-free paper

On the cover: The Shakers of New Lebanon, New York, Religious Exercises in
the Meeting-house by Joseph Becker.

Frontispiece: Two Shaker sisters at Canterbury, New Hampshire, display their
saxophones. Members of alternative religions do not always conform to uninformed
stereotypes. These religious women obviously enjoy secular music.

To many friends among members of alternative religions

CONTENTS

PREFACE

The citizens of the founding generation of the United States dissented from English rule and boldly asserted their independence. The Declaration of Independence gave voice to the political aspirations of those who rebelled against a parliament that taxed colonists who had no representation in those proceedings. The U.S. Constitution, crafted after the turmoil of warfare and an era of political disunity, sought to secure peace and unity and to guarantee fundamental liberties, including the free exercise of religion. Dissent in a political context has been an honored tradition in America, and we celebrate the founders as patriots.

But Americans have not uniformly celebrated communities of religious dissent, endorsed in the Constitution by the principle of the free exercise of religion. On the contrary, the public expression of religious dissent has often resulted in opposition. People, whose views or practices differ from dominant religious patterns in American society, frequently have been the target of ridicule, harassment, and persecution. Rarely have such religious dissenters been accorded the honor that Americans regularly heap upon political dissenters.

The contrasting public images of the two different forms of dissent, political and religious, are evident in the simple juxtaposition of pairs of political and religious dissenters Thomas Paine and Ann Lee, Frederick Douglass and John Humphrey Noyes, Jane Addams and Mary Baker Eddy, Ralph Nader and David Koresh. American historians have widely celebrated the first person in each of these pairs for his or her pioneering efforts on behalf of, respectively, political liberty, the abolition of slavery, assistance to the urban poor, and protection of the environment. The second half of each pair experienced bitter opposition: Lee was physically assaulted by angry mobs in several New England towns; Noyes was run out of the country by clergy, who hoped to bring him into criminal court; Eddy was the target of vilification by former students as well as lawyers and ministers; and Koresh was harassed by the government. Moreover, historians, looking back on the roles of these religious dissenters, have often failed to offer balanced accounts of their lives.

Why have religious dissenters so often attracted the ire and hostility of others? What motivates those who attack such dissenters? What can we gain by learning more about the diverse communities of religious dissent that have been a part of American history from its earliest days? What role have these communities played in our national story, and what may we expect in the years ahead?

The chapters that follow employ a variety of terms used to identify and define religious communities of dissent. Some of these terms, including "cult" and "sect," have long traditions of use, stretching back to the centuries when Latin was the official language of scholars. But the meanings of words often change over time; and terms that once were neutral or simply descriptive sometimes take on harshly negative implications and potentially lose their original usefulness, including the two just mentioned. Other terms have been coined more recently to circumvent the stereotypes associated with older categories. Among this newer terminology are "outsider groups" and "New Religious Movements." Sometimes the newer nomenclature is useful despite certain limitations. "Marginal religious communities," for example, is a positional designation—not a qualitative judgment—implying a location on the margin or edge of mainstream religious groups. When using these terms, it is important to recognize that they are often loaded with powerful assumptions and implications.

Often people who attack religious dissenters are ignorant of the ideas and practices of those whom they attack. Sometimes the attackers imagine that the people who hold the alleged religious views or engage in the ascribed spiritual practices are dangerous and threatening to the attackers' own religious values. Ignorance and misunderstanding regularly fuel uninformed responses—whether hateful feelings, verbal threats, or physical assaults.

Confronting someone whose religious commitments are different may challenge our own way of life, our deepest values, and our most fundamental views. Religion, when learned at the knees of parents or from clergy who appear to be guardians of truth, is deeply ingrained and many times unexamined. As long as those around us hold similar views and participate in similar practices, we are not forced to examine and evaluate our own assumptions and beliefs. But when we discover, either through personal encounter or through formal education, that not everyone holds the same beliefs or follows the same practices, we are often provoked to examine our own views.

This discovery of religious diversity can be frightening and threatening; it can fuel feelings of defensiveness and aggression. It can also be exhilarating and liberating and open a fascinating window on a new world. Either way, we tend to assume that the dissenter is an outsider. We prefer to assume that our religious beliefs and practices are in the mainstream, and therefore we have little need to justify them. We find it reassuring to locate ourselves amongst the majority. In such a situation, dissent takes on, almost by definition, a negative cast as a less legitimate position.

This is the point at which the narrative in this volume— the story of the rich tradition of communities of religious dissent throughout American history—has something to offer. This narrative relates the engaging story of bold men and women who affirmed their deepest religious values, often in the face of physical hardship and overt hostility. Motivated by religious values and convinced of the truthfulness of their spiritual claims, these dissenters bravely faced opposition, and in most cases, the difficulties they confronted did not deter them. For them religion was a reassuring force and power that enabled them to perform under distress or hardship.

This narrative also documents the impact of the First Amendment to the U.S. Constitution on religious dissenters and all Americans. Its guarantee of the free exercise of religion has enshrined in our nation the right of individuals to hold diverse religious beliefs and to practice different religions. The constitutional principle of free exercise allows Americans to agree to disagree about religion and to provide sanctuary for religious dissenters. This book illustrates the rich variety of ways that Americans have chosen to be religious and the distinctive ideas and practices that have developed as expressions of their beliefs.

But this story of America's communities of dissent is important beyond the interesting people who fill its pages. In this story there are grounds for celebrating religious dissenters as well as political dissenters. As the story of religious dissent unfolds from the time of the earliest settlements up to the present, we must recognize that the religious dissenters have played the role of legal pioneers for all of us in their pursuit of religious liberty.

With the passage of time, the number of dissenting religious communities in the United States has grown exponentially. This book is by necessity highly selective, and it attempts only to tell the story of some representative or especially prominent communities of dissent. There is no absolute way to number how many such groups have existed in American history. There is, however, clear evidence that as each year passes, the number of such communities rises. One factor contributing to this increase is the change in the national immigration policy in 1965 which has facilitated the importation of diverse religious communities from abroad.

By their actions on behalf of their own communities and their efforts to secure their own rights in the face of opposition, religious dissenters have broadened the religious liberties enjoyed by all Americans. As the courts, for example, have moved to support the claims of dissenting communities to exist or to practice their beliefs, those actions initiated by religious dissenters in the name of self-defense or self-preservation have had the practical effect of enhancing the religious liberties of all Americans. This story therefore is a part of our national epic.

COMMUNITIES OF DISSENT

Talking About
Religious Outsiders

H ow do you respond to people who are different? What is your reaction when you meet individuals who belong to religious communities whose beliefs you do not understand? Why do we often feel uncomfortable when we encounter belief systems that we do not share or religiously motivated behavior that is unusual? Is there a way to talk about such groups that is both accurate and fair? These are questions we will explore in this book as we focus on the lesser-known, and sometimes controversial, religious traditions of the United States.

Let's begin with an example of an alternative religion—which is one name applied to such groups. Admittedly, Isaac Bullard and his disciples—the Vermont Pilgrims—were very different from their neighbors in 1817 in the area of Woodstock, Vermont. Many expressed shock and disgust upon first seeing Bullard and his small band of followers. One observer writing in September of that year called their appearance "very singular." They wore "long beards, close caps, and bearskins tied around them." Bullard himself sported a long red beard. This same observer, whose account was published in a local newspaper, branded the Vermont Pilgrims as "deluded."

Bullard, called the Prophet by his followers, dominated the life of the community. He professed to receive divine revelations that were the basis of his religious ideas and the behavior required of members. The Prophet denounced the established churches of the day as corrupt and sinful. He hoped to restore a pure and simple Christianity, free of creeds, rituals, and sacraments.

The Prophet made heavy demands on his followers. The Vermont Pilgrims were to seek perfection by living a life of poverty and self-denial. Bullard required them to give up luxuries in dress and food. Sometimes they wore coarse sackcloth instead of bearskins. They fasted constantly. The central item in their diet was gruel, or mush, composed of water or milk and flour. They rarely ate meat and rejected other basic practices of Western civilization, declaring them sinful inventions. They gave up, for example, the use of knives and forks as well as conventional furniture, preferring to suck their food from a common bowl through cane stalks while standing. Based on Bullard's reading of the Bible, they neither bathed nor cut their hair.

These practices, revolting as they seemed to others, were considered steps toward holiness by the Vermont Pilgrims. They hoped to avoid sin through such customs. Sometimes they rolled in the dust as an act of humility and repentance. They also chanted strange refrains, such as: "My God, my God, my God, my God, What wouldst thou have me do? Mummyjum, mummyjum, mummyjum, mummyjum."

The Vermont Pilgrims, not surprisingly, attracted ridicule and opposition. As a result Bullard led his small community, numbering at the height of its popularity perhaps forty members, out of Vermont and on a journey westward that ended for a remaining handful of followers in 1819 in the newly formed Arkansas Territory. On that trip the "Mummyjums," as opponents dubbed them, were subject to repeated hostility and physical abuse. The last recorded reference to the group was in 1824, when one traveler visited briefly with two members living in a hut on the banks of the Mississippi River.

The Vermont Pilgrims are only a footnote in the pages of religious history, but they embody patterns typical of alternative religious communities in the United States. These patterns will be discussed further, but first we must confront the fact that a variety of terms exists for such groups. Some of the labels commonly used to categorize or describe alternative, or "alternate," religions carry very negative implications. If the Vermont Pilgrims were active today, the media would call them a *cult*, which for many is a term of deliberate condemnation. Those who use it intend to depict the group under discussion as extreme, radical, and fanatical. Use of the category *cult* becomes one way for people to separate themselves from others, to draw boundaries, to identify insiders and outsiders.

Originally the term *cult* had a positive meaning. The Latin root *colere*, from which *cult* derives, means simply "to tend or till." Cognate, or related, words include *culture, cultivate,* and *cultigen*—all of which have extremely positive meanings. One specific related notion involves the concept of tending or caring for a deity or god. Thus *cult* sometimes refers in particular to the structured worship of God. In that sense historians and sociologists use the term, without prejudice, to describe communities that share a pattern of religious worship. Therefore the word *cult* need not be a negative reference.

Another term used for alternative religions—*sect*—also has negative implications for many. Commentators often distinguish sects from mainline, or mainstream, religions. By that usage they imply that sects are less acceptable than mainstream religions or less legitimate than large established religious communities. Often they depict sectarian groups as deviant or dangerous. Again we have lost the original meaning of the term. *Sect* derives from the Latin verb *sequi*, meaning "to follow." A *sect* can be defined positively as a community that *follows* a particular leader, ideology, or program. It, too, need not be a term of derision.

Therefore it is possible to describe the Vermont Pilgrims as a cult or a sect in a positive manner. In this book we will use such terms from time to time without any negative implications, reaching back to their original meanings. Only in the mouths of others will we allow such terms to carry negative connotations.

Because these terms have acquired such negative values, historians and sociologists who study such communities have developed a number of substitute categories. Several deserve special mention because they add to our understanding of such groups.

Two of these—*alternative religions* and *alternate religious traditions*—imply that the communities under discussion are not prevalent or dominant in society. Implicit in these categories is the notion that those who join such groups have chosen to do so as a protest against mainstream religion.

Outsider religious groups is another term employed for cults and sects. The political implications of this term are obvious. It draws a line between insiders and outsiders, thereby suggesting that the former control society's institutions of power and influence whereas the latter stand outside those institutions. In most societies there is little doubt on the part of either group who is inside and who is outside. Outsiders know that they are outsiders because of their relations with insiders.

Another category often used for these groups is *marginal communities*. This terminology draws its meaning from the notion that society has a center, and there are edges, or margins, too. Those groups occupying the center define the entity; those located on the margins are peripheral to the definition. Again power and control enter into the formula implied in this language.

We should be alert, however, to the possibility that some alternative religious communities identified as outsiders or classified as marginal may seek out that classification intentionally. There are times when the margin or edges of society function as places of refuge and security for groups that do not enjoy widespread esteem or respect. They may, in fact, seek out such locations as a strategy for survival or regrouping.

One final term recently used for these groups, especially by sociologists, is *New Religious Movements* (NRMs). This category is a useful reminder that cults and sects often arise anew out of changing historical circumstances. Many such groups do not have long histories reaching to the ancient past. To put the matter another way, NRMs are born in every age. There is no limit to the possible number of alternative religions.

All of this terminology—from the established language to the newest categories—points in different ways to the defining feature of such groups, namely, dissent from prevailing religious patterns. *Dissent* involves conscious difference or disagreement.

The Vermont Pilgrims chose to be different from their neighbors. Isaac Bullard and his followers made a decision to live an impoverished, unclean lifestyle. Their behavior set them apart from those who lived in more conventional ways. There is no doubt that they determined to follow a course of action identifying themselves as outsiders. Their behavior established clear boundaries between their community and others. Those boundaries worked to the advantage of members of the community as well as to their opponents'. Finally Bullard traveled to the geographical margins of U.S. society in the West, perhaps in part to secure a location where his followers might live as they pleased. In 1817 the Vermont Pilgrims were a New Religious Movement.

One other category needs to be introduced into our discussion of the language used to describe alternative religious communities. It is commonplace to talk about the "other" and thereby intend something different from ourselves. The concept of "otherness" is a shorthand way of separating the speaker from those being discussed. It sets up a situation of "us" and "them." It is nearly impossible to talk or write about religious groups different from our own without involving some sense of otherness. At the start, therefore, we must acknowledge that this is the situation for all of us with nearly every group that follows, not just with the Vermont Pilgrims.

This volume attempts to discuss the "other" in an even-handed and fair manner. That requires us to examine carefully the self-representations of alternative religious movements while at the same time we look closely at the criticisms rendered by those who are not part of these communities. The fact that these groups constitute the other for most of us does not mean we cannot obtain a clear understanding of them. The goal of the historian is not to declare one or another religious group to be "true" and all others "false," but rather to understand the ways these communities have functioned in the lives of their members and the roles they have played in the story of our nation. These are the objectives of this book.

In the chapters that follow we examine select examples of alternative religions drawn from the full chronological sweep of American history. The story divides into three time periods, corresponding to the colonial era, the nineteenth century, and the twentieth century. In each we see NRMs arise, play significant roles as dissenting communities, and follow one of several possible evolutionary paths.

Many of these groups, led by a powerful religious leader, appear at a particular historical moment, struggle or thrive for a limited time, and then pass from the scene, often shortly after the death of the founder. In fact, if we were to rely solely on numbers, it would be safe to suggest that the majority of NRMs have followed this developmental scheme. Some dissenting religious communities manage to rise, flourish, and survive the death of their founder, only to be absorbed by the society they were protesting. In these cases, accommodation led to the loss of identity and to a different kind of death. Finally, relatively few NRMs arise, thrive during the founding and succeeding generations, build lasting structures and institutions that allow them to exist within the larger society, and manage to retain their distinctive dissenting proclamation or reason for existence. But some have risen to great local power and influence.

The colonial period in American history was a first time of growth for NRMs in the New World. European settlers, attracted by the reports of the early explorers and the prospects of abundant land, economic opportunity, refuge from hostile forces, a new life, and freedom to believe and worship as they saw fit, came to the eastern shores of North America intent on establishing themselves in this environment. The context proved especially attractive to those who were denied religious freedom in their homelands.

Settlers in every part of the English colonies had come with the hope of practicing their religion without interference or persecution. Ironically, sometimes those who sought tolerance in the New World proved intolerant of others. As a result the colonial period witnessed both the introduction of alternative religions from Europe and the emergence of NRMs from within the colonial settlements. Once again there were religious insiders and outsiders. The New World proved a haven for only some dissenters; others found themselves on the margins yet again.

The nineteenth century was a time of immense religious innovation in the United States, fostered in part by the constitutional principle of the free exercise of religion adopted by the new nation following the Revolutionary War. That principle, alongside the prohibition of an established state religion, opened the door to the free marketplace of religious ideas and to competition among religious groups throughout the United States.

The geographical expansion of the young nation across the continent resulted in vast areas of land being added to the country. This open space, perceived to be empty despite the presence of Native Americans, proved inviting to those who wished to experiment with new forms of society. This expanding nation attracted immigrants in large numbers. Some were conventional in religious outlook, but others welcomed the opportunity to explore new ways of being religious. The nineteenth century celebrated individualism, the pioneering spirit, and the notion of a free democratic society. The logic of these ideals supported those who sought to be different in matters of religious faith and practice. The result at that time was a wave of religious experimentation and the growth of many New Religious Movements.

The twentieth century has continued the pattern of religious innovation and the emergence of large numbers of alternative religions, some born in reaction to hostility and persecution, despite the constitutional guarantees of religious freedom, others the product of the nation's growing cultural and ethnic diversity. Whereas the earliest centuries of the American experience witnessed the influx of immigrants from western Europe and Africa, the twentieth century saw rising numbers pour into the United States from eastern Europe, the Middle East, Asia, and areas south of our border, bringing with them religious traditions from their homelands. Sometimes these traditions spawned NRMs in the new environment; other times hybrids developed, blending old and new ideas. The pace of religious innovation has not slowed. In fact, the turn of the millennium has been a further powerful stimulus toward innovation in the United States.

There is little reason to believe that the United States will ever see an end to the formation of NRMs. On the contrary, an increasingly diverse population, the interaction of countless traditions, and the political climate created by the principle of religious freedom almost guarantee that Americans will see even more alternative religions. That makes it all the more important that we attempt to understand such groups.

Why do NRMs attract so many Americans? After all, protesters seldom win popularity contests, no matter what the circumstances. Religious dissenters are no exception to that rule. They, too, suffer at the hands of popular opinion. Cults and sects frequently appear as threatening, frightening, or at least suspicious. So why would Americans choose to join religious communities that are viewed in this way? That question is one of the major concerns we will address throughout this book.

Dissent is not by definition a bad thing. Much of our nation's history is the positive product of dissent. The nation's founders protested unfair governance by England, revolted, and created a democratic society. The antislavery movement of the first half of the nineteenth century protested against the buying and selling of Africans as slaves and ultimately brought an end to that evil practice. Twentieth-century advocates of the civil rights movement and equal opportunity have lobbied against discriminatory laws and unfair economic practices in an effort to create a just society. Dissent is and always has been an honored principle in U.S. life. Religious dissenters have played no small part in cultivating respect for that principle.

And yet, as we will see, religious dissenters have suffered immensely at the hands of insiders or the mainstream. They have experienced ridicule, harassment, hostility, persecution, and even death at the hands of their opponents. Too frequently Americans have not lived up to the ideals embodied in the Constitution that call for the creation of a tolerant, free society with opportunity for religious diversity. And yet the United States has continued to attract NRMs to its shores and to give rise to others from within it. The United States has been a fertile seedbed for outsider religious communities.

As the story of America's alternative religious movements unfolds, watch for common patterns in many of the groups, including the role of the founder or first leader of the community; the importance attached to the Bible, other scriptures, or special revelations; the unique religious beliefs or ideas that set the group apart; the distinctive religious practices that mark the boundaries of the community; and the unique institutions established by it. In addition, pay particular attention to society's reactions to an alternative religious group, the group's negative judgments against mainstream churches, the fate of its community following the death of its founder, and its present situation.

The following chapters focus on particular groupings of select alternative religious movements in different time periods. The choices made for each period illustrate some—not all—of the most prominent patterns of dissenting religious groups. No attempt is made to be comprehensive. Scores of other communities might enter this narrative, but the limits of space make their exploration impossible. Success is also not the criterion for inclusion. Some alternative groups discussed in the following chapters have become powerful denominations in the United States, but many more have passed from the scene. This book describes the rich tradition of alternative religions in the United States and the role they have played in the lives of their members and in the story of our nation.

*The antics of the Mummyjums, or followers of Isaac Bullard,
attracted attention from all who saw them as they traveled from
Vermont to the West in 1817. Their itinerary included a stop in
August at the Shaker village in New Lebanon, New York,
where they demonstrated their public opposition to Shaker society. An anonymous observer in that community took note in a
journal of the Pilgrims' strange appearance and behavior,
including their refusal to accept offers of hospitality.*

Some part of them were married people, and had their
families with them; others were unmarried, young people
and children who had followed their parents. Bullard the
prophet had his wife along with him, with an infant child,
which they affirmed to be a holy child, and called his name
Christ, or the Second Christ. They walked back & forth
through our street most of the day, with a very short staff
in each hand; so that they were obliged to walk with their
bodies bent in an horizontal position, which with their
long beards, odd grimaces, incoherent language, and singular manoeuvres, gave them a very ludicrous appearance.
They were very severe in their censures against our
Society, prophesied judgments upon us, and uttered many
curses against us. Yet they were treated very kindly, had
victuals offered them freely, and as they staid overnight,
the Deacons kindly offered them lodging, provided their
males & females would agree to lodge in separate apart-
ments. This offer they rejected with much contempt,

& took their lodging in the street, under a large spreading willow, near one of our dwellings. They also rejected all our offers of victuals, and even our offers to feed their team of a yoke of oxen & horse, attached to a cart which contained their baggage; but tied the poor beasts up, fasting from mere contempt of our kind offers; because we could not indulge them in lodging promiscuously with their women. When they left us they bent their course to the South. . . .

CHAPTER ONE

Early Dissenters and Popular Religion

The Puritans who settled the Massachusetts Bay Colony in 1630 were dissenters from the Church of England, or Anglicanism. But they had little tolerance for those who did not agree with all aspects of Puritan doctrine and religious practice. In the first decade of the colony's history no individual was more outspoken in his criticism of such intolerance than Roger Williams, the founder of Rhode Island.

Williams did not come to the New World intending to establish a separate colony. On the contrary, this Puritan clergyman who held a degree from Cambridge University arrived in Boston in early 1631 expecting to serve as the minister of a Puritan congregation. That plan did not work out, however, because Williams criticized the Boston congregation for failing to separate completely from the Church of England. He regarded the Puritans in Massachusetts as tainted by their unwillingness to declare a complete separation.

Williams not only believed that the Puritans must renounce all links with the Anglican Church. He also denied the authority of Puritan magistrates, or civil leaders, to enforce religious regulations on the colonists in Massachusetts. In other words, he called for the complete separation of church and state in New England. At that time there was no precedent for such views either in England or New England, or for that matter anywhere in Europe. In the seventeenth century it was commonplace for church and state to be closely linked and to reinforce each other's rules and regulations. The church preached obedience to civil leaders and to established laws, and the state enforced rules and regulations concerning religious worship and moral values. That was the situation in early New England.

Puritan ministers emphasized the responsibility of citizens to obey the magistrates and to live as law-abiding members of society. The magistrates in New England prosecuted and punished individuals who did not attend services regularly or who violated accepted patterns of conduct and ethical behavior. Ministers and magistrates worked in tandem to enforce both religious and civil regulations. Those who dared to defy this powerful coalition felt the full force of both parties. Roger Williams experienced this dual disciplinary action.

Williams also criticized the Massachusetts Bay Colony's claim to the lands it occupied. He believed that the founders of the colony had acted inappropriately in seizing territory from the Native Americans who had inhabited it for centuries. He declared the charter from the king of England insufficient grounds for possession of the territory. Therefore in his judgment the Puritans' title to the land was invalid. As an alternative approach, Williams proposed that the settlers negotiate directly with the Indians for the land.

Williams's dissenting views were no small matter to the colonists, who possessed a very high sense of their own mission. Many believed that they had been chosen by God to come to New England to create a godly society that would serve as a model for England. John Winthrop, the first governor of the Massachusetts Bay Colony, had spoken in 1630 of the Puritans' responsibility to establish "a city on a hill" that might serve as a prototype for others to emulate. Williams's attack on the manner in which the Puritans had taken possession of the land constituted a radical challenge to the New England way of doing things.

By late 1635 the leadership of the Bay Colony had experienced quite enough criticism and public dissent from Williams. The Puritans may have left England in order to establish a better society that would enable them to worship God as they saw fit, but they were not prepared to allow one of their own the right to criticize the New England way or the freedom to do things differently. The Puritans who had been religious outsiders in England became the insiders in New England. They, in turn, were not willing to tolerate religious critics, or outsiders, within their ranks. Therefore the General Court of Massachusetts, the legislative body of the colony, banished Williams in October. But before he could be deported to England, he fled to territory south of Massachusetts and the following summer founded the settlement of Providence on the Narragansett Bay, which would ultimately become Rhode Island.

Williams tried to create a different kind of society from that in Massachusetts. He negotiated with Native Americans and purchased land from them. He was one of the first in New England to become a friend to the natives and to learn their language. In his colony, which grew slowly, he established what he called soul liberty, the principle that religion does not require uniformity and conformity. In other words, he took a

17

stand for religious freedom, liberty of a kind that was almost unheard of at that time in the Western world. The standard approach to such matters had called for rigid conformity by citizens to the religious views of the ruler, whether the ruling party was a king, a legislative body, or a religious faction. Williams was ahead of his time on the matter of religious freedom.

Eventually Williams traveled to London to secure a formal charter from Parliament. The charter he brought back in 1644 combined the towns in the region into the Providence Plantations. Three years later a group of residents established what they called a democratical form of government for the colony that guaranteed religious liberty to its inhabitants. They affirmed the principle that "all men may walk as their consciences persuade them, every one in the name of his God." Roger Williams became an outspoken advocate for religious liberty. He published extensively in defense of the principle of toleration and against the use of force in matters of religion. Coercion, he said—even physical persecution—does not produce belief or true religion.

Williams's religious evolution did not end with his protest against the Puritan religious establishment in the Bay Colony. Within a few years of his banishment from Massachusetts, he became convinced that the religious views of the Baptists were correct. The distinguishing mark of Baptists was their belief that the sacrament of baptism, the ritual application of water to new members of the church, must be restricted to those old enough to testify personally to their faith in Christ. Infants therefore must not be baptized. Baptists also believed that the true church was a voluntary association, not a community constituted by the state. Williams had a hand in forming the first Baptist congregation in America in 1639.

A few months later, however, he disavowed that new commitment and left the Baptists. Now he declared himself a "seeker," one who was looking for the true church. He thought that the model for the authentic church was in the New Testament, but no organized community in his day lived up to that high ideal. Williams never gave up his commitment to soul liberty or the separation of church and state, but he also never found a religious community that met his standards. He remained a seeker throughout the balance of his life, dissenting from all organized religious communities.

Roger Williams is an excellent example of the principle of religious dissent carried to an extreme. He rejected all organized religious groups and finally practiced his faith in isolation. He also anticipated the dissenting pattern of scores of small religious groups during the colonial period.

Other dissenters in colonial America shared Williams's uneasiness with established religious patterns. Scattered throughout the English colonies, they often gave rise to some of the first NRMs in America.

One contemporary of Williams who also challenged the Puritan leadership in Massachusetts was Anne Hutchinson, a talented woman who came to the colony in 1634. She was a devout follower of the Puritan minister John Cotton. In Boston she began to convene weekly meetings to discuss Cotton's sermons. Soon she was criticizing ministers other than Cotton, charging them with overemphasizing the role of good works or ethical actions in salvation. She attracted increasingly large numbers to her home, and soon this "Hutchinsonian" faction was disrupting established religious patterns and threatening the authority of the clergy. It was particularly offensive to male ministers that a woman would dare to challenge them.

19

In a later period Hutchinson and her followers would have been called a cult and charged with religious extremism. In Puritan Boston she and her disciples found themselves accused of heresy, or the teaching of false doctrine. Her opponents, including the ministers of the colony, with the exception of Cotton and her brother-in-law John Wheelwright, condemned her religious views in a formal gathering of the clergy in 1637. When she was pressed to explain on what authority her views rested, Hutchinson acknowledged that she had received direct revelations from God. Puritan leaders believed God's will was communicated only through the Bible as interpreted by the clergy, not through visions or revelations to individuals. On the basis of this belief, the civil authorities, led by John Winthrop, tried Hutchinson and, after conviction, banished her. In 1638 Hutchinson left Massachusetts for the region that later became Rhode Island. In 1643 she died on Long Island in an Indian conflict. The controversy surrounding her revealed once again early New England's intolerance of dissent.

Samuel Gorton, another religious radical in early New England, experienced repeated hostility from the Puritan leadership. His dissent included a general attack on all clerical authority. A tailor by trade, Gorton came to New England during the height of the crisis precipitated by Anne Hutchinson. Although he did not take part in that controversy, he was later accused of uncivil behavior and deviant religious opinions. Wherever he moved—Boston, Plymouth, Providence—he aroused opposition from those in authority—even from Roger Williams. In Plymouth, for example, he was tried for insubordination and banished. In Providence his verbal assaults on ministers and his general attack on Puritan authority led to a request for assistance and ultimately to an expeditionary force that moved against the Gortonists, as his followers were called, in the area south of Providence. They were brought to Boston, tried, convicted of heresy and crimes against the government, and sentenced to hard labor. A few months later, in 1644, the General Court overturned those convictions, and Gorton traveled to England to lodge complaints against the Puritans. He later returned to New England, where he spent the rest of his life without further incident.

But it was not simply English-speaking individuals in New England who found themselves cast as dissenters. Numerous settlers from other European countries also protested against the prevailing religious patterns in the English colonies. Pieter Plockhoy, a Mennonite, or follower of the Dutch Protestant leader Menno Simons, born in the Netherlands, established a short-lived community in 1663 near the mouth of the Delaware River in the Middle Colonies. The plan for that community reflected Plockhoy's social and religious ideas. Plockhoy, who had lived and traveled in Europe, hoped to reform the Mennonite movement, making it more responsive to the poor. He aroused opposition in both the Netherlands and England because of his commitment to simplicity, pacifism, and social justice.

In 1659 Plockhoy published *A Way Propounded to Make the Poor in These and Other Nations Happy*, his blueprint for an ideal society based on love, harmony, and the rule of God's spirit. He and some forty followers hoped to build such a community on the lower Delaware. Their vision included a society free from unrest and intolerance, in which all shared the wealth and the goods. Unfortunately, the Quaking Society of Plockhoy, as the group was called by some, had little opportunity to conduct their experiment. In 1664 English military forces

21

destroyed all the Dutch settlements along the river, including Zwaanendael, the name of their site. Though Plockhoy remained in the Delaware region for thirty more years, he ultimately died penniless, blind, and frustrated both religiously and socially.

The case of Conrad Beissel, a German mystic and religious seeker, is somewhat different. Orphaned at an early age, Beissel worked at various occupations and became affiliated with a series of different religious groups. In 1720 he came to Pennsylvania, where he hoped to find a religious community that would fulfill his needs but was thwarted. For a time he was a member of the German Baptist Brethren, or Dunkers, and even served as a minister, but he split with that group and in 1732 founded the Ephrata Community, also known as the Cloister, in Lancaster County, Pennsylvania.

Under Beissel's leadership and influenced by the revelations he said he experienced, Ephrata prospered for several decades, having some two hundred members in the 1750s. The members resembled a monastic community in several ways, with some of the men and the women living separately and abstaining from sexual relations. Among their other distinctive beliefs were worship on Saturday instead of Sunday, baptism by immersion rather than by sprinkling, and pacifism or nonresistance to violence. The community placed a high value on education, music, and devotional art. Ephrata managed to survive for more than forty years after Beissel's death before disbanding in 1814.

One example of an alternative religious group in the South demonstrates that no section of the English colonies was immune from radical religion. The dissenters were members of the Dutartre family, who were most likely descendants of Huguenots, French Protestants driven out of France by their Roman Catholic opponents. A substantial number took refuge in Charleston, South Carolina, which by the beginning of the eighteenth century had acquired a reputation for harboring religious dissenters.

Members of the Dutartre family came under the influence of such religious radicals and decided to withdraw from all organized churches. They declared their family to be uniquely chosen by God as a holy family, which, as in the days of biblical Noah, was selected to start the world anew when God chose to destroy the wicked human race. Members of the family used private revelations from God to justify a bigamous relationship that resulted in charges of adultery. They rejected civil authority, refusing to obey South Carolina's laws. When authorities attempted to arrest them, an armed confrontation followed, and the Dutartres killed a judge. After the militia subdued and arrested the family, they were tried and convicted of immorality, rebellion, and murder. The Dutartres remained defiant, confident that God had chosen them as prophets and would vindicate them. Ultimately, three family members were executed before two others confessed their errors and escaped the gallows. This episode confirmed for many the threat posed by religious radicals.

It is difficult, if not impossible, to generalize about these religious outsiders in the colonial period. Each of the individuals or groups held distinctive ideas based on private revelations, visions, unique interpretations of the Bible, or other grounds. They would not have viewed each other as allies. What they shared was their dissenting stance against the dominant religious, social, and political patterns. They stood outside conventional religious organizations. They knew they were outsiders, and they knew exactly where the boundaries were that separated them from others.

The world of magic represented another kind of alternative religious activity. In its broadest sense, magic refers to a wide variety of practices that purported to manipulate occult or hidden forces for good or evil. Magic was the realm of witches, wizards, folk healers, Native American shamans, African-American conjurers, and others knowledgeable about such matters. The world of magic was not remote from daily life in the colonies. It often intersected directly with sickness and healing, predicting the weather, finding lost objects, explaining the unexplainable, calculating favorable times for action, seeking good luck, and protecting against or harming enemies—to cite but a few of its possible uses. Magic existed alongside the conventional churches as an alternative source of power. Individuals active in the churches also consulted with those knowledgeable about these alternative traditions. Magic and the occult were not only the province of outsiders.

The use of magic for healing was one of its most common applications. In the colonial period people frequently consulted conjurers or cunning people to deal with sickness or disease. Charms and spells provided remedies for a variety of ills. Those in possession of specialized knowledge, for example, concocted and mixed powders that could be used to cure both physical and mental disorders. Some potions involved secret, unwritten formulas only. In 1684 Increase Mather, a distinguished Puritan clergyman in Boston, described one such charm in his *Essay for the Recording of Illustrious Providences:*

Not long since a Man left with another in this Town, as
a rare secret a cure for the Ague, which was this: five
letters, viz. x, a, etc., were to be written successively on
pieces of Bread and given to the Patient, on one piece
he must write the word *Kalendant*, and so on another
the next day, and in five days (if he did believe) he
should not fail of cure.

Mather did not approve the use of this cure. But people
looking for healthfulness were willing both to pray to God and
to pay persons who claimed to possess healing powers.

The principal opponents of the use of magic in daily life
were members of the clergy such as Mather. They assumed
that many who employed magic for one reason or another did
so because they were ignorant and unaware of the full implications of their actions. Ministers attempted to convince their
congregations that magic was inescapably linked with the
workings of the devil. Even "white magic," or magic that
worked positive results, was toying with the forces of Satan.
The clergy declared that such seemingly innocent traditional
practices as using a sieve or a key to discover the location of
lost items—whether they worked or not—involved a pact with
evil. Despite persistent criticism by the clergy, such practices
were apparently widespread throughout the colonies.

The Salem witchcraft trials of 1692 became the most celebrated episode in colonial history involving magic or the
occult. This episode began with the playful curiosity of young
girls who wanted to see into the future. When their actions
were discovered, they began a process of naming witches in
their midst. Fueled by the suggestion of Samuel Parris, the
local minister, that witches might be close at hand, local panic

and hysteria set in as the accusations multiplied. The people most often accused of being witches were outsiders, especially older women, who were particularly vulnerable. Before this contagion was stopped, the jails were overflowing. The accusations did not rest on conventional rules of evidence and testimony. As a result twenty-four people died, nineteen by hanging, before the governor brought an end to these proceedings.

One of those accused of witchcraft early in the Salem experience was Tituba, an American Indian slave, not an African as previously assumed by many historians. She and her Indian husband, John, were the property of the minister Samuel Parris. It appears that Tituba was brought to Massachusetts from Barbados. When the activities of the young girls, which included one of Parris's daughters, came to public light and attempts were made to counter the influence of magic, Tituba became involved in one of the countermagic efforts, which led to an accusation of witchcraft against her. After an initial denial of the accusation, Tituba confessed to a pact with the devil and to plotting harm to the children who had testified to the anguish and physical pain they had experienced. She gave a detailed account and implicated others in the narrative, a confession she later recanted. Tituba escaped execution through her confession.

Another outsider caught in the web of accusations spun by the girls and subsequently by Tituba was Sarah Good, the daughter of a once prosperous innkeeper in Wenham who was impoverished by the time of the hysteria. She was one of the first people accused by the girls. Good, who was thirty-eight years old (considered middle age at the time), had a reputation for being abrasive and often quarrelsome. She appeared haggard, and she was known for having a sharp tongue. She also was not a faithful churchgoer. When Good was charged with being familiar with evil spirits, she denied completely all the accusations. She excused her infrequent church attendance by pleading poverty and inappropriate clothing. During her examination the girls cried out that Good was torturing them at that very moment. Her denial and protestations were in vain. She was tried, convicted, and executed on July 19, 1692.

One of the most prominent Puritan ministers of the period was Cotton Mather, pastor of the Second Church (Old North) in Boston and the son of Increase. He was a vigorous opponent of witchcraft, a position he made plain in his publications on the subject before the outbreak in Salem. Late in 1692 Mather published his judgments about those events in a volume entitled *Wonders of the Invisible World*. This book, hastily written, was his attempt to extract some useful purpose from the diabolical happenings. He defended the methods of the court and tried to assure his readers about the procedures being employed. At the time Mather was willing to accept the notion of spectral evidence as sufficient to convict, though he had growing cause for concern about it. Spectral evidence rested on the accuser's testimony that the apparition, or spirit form, of the accused had tortured or assaulted the accuser. Spectral testimony was not subject to the independent confirmation required of conventional accusations. Because of his strong conviction that the devil was behind the outburst in Salem and because he never doubted the reality of witchcraft, Mather was willing to consider spectral evidence, despite certain reservations. His publication about Salem appeared almost at the same moment that the governor brought an end to the proceedings.

The Salem witch trials stand as evidence of the presence of the occult in early America. Although the tragic events in Salem were unusual, they confirm the widespread belief in magic and alternative spiritual practices. Interest in the occult did not disappear after Salem, though it frequently took other forms. For example, the colonists regularly consulted almanacs for astrological information. Almanacs published in the colonies included horoscopes as well as astrological tables and traditional lore related to the best days for planting crops and gardens, conducting business, taking a trip, or engaging in a host of other activities. There was no reduction of interest in consulting wise people who could heal through occult means. The practice of medicine at the time was extremely primitive. Consulting folk healers, or cunning people, a name given to those skilled in such matters, was no more dangerous or life-threatening than being attended by a physician.

It is difficult to document the full extent of magic and the occult in colonial America. Yet such practices were a significant part of the alternative spiritual world outside established religious denominations.

The most controversial aspect of the legal proceedings at the witchcraft trials in Salem involved the admission of spectral evidence provided by witnesses testifying that the spirit form of the accused had tortured or assaulted the accusers. The false accusation against Sarah Good illustrates the problem. In her case the accuser was caught in a lie, but the ultimate outcome did not change. She was convicted and executed. At her execution Good defiantly maintained her innocence when challenged by the minister Nicholas Noyes, and before her death she warned that he would pay for his actions.

The 30th of June, the Court according to Adjournment again sat; five more were tried, *viz.* Sarah Good and Rebecca Nurse of Salem Village; Susanna Martin of Amsbury; Elizabeth How of Ipswich; and Sarah Wildes of Topsfield; these were all condemned that Sessions, and were all Executed on the 19th of July.

At the Tryal of Sarah Good, one of the afflicted fell in a Fit, and after coming out of it, she cried out of the Prisoner, for stabing her in the breast with a Knife, and that she had broken the Knife in stabbing of her, accordingly a piece of the blade of a Knife was found about her. Immediately information being given to the Court, a young Man was called, who produced a Shaft and part of the Blade, which the Court having viewed and compared, saw it to be the same. And upon inquiry the young Man affirmed, that yesterday he happened to break that Knife, and that he cast away the upper part, this afflicted person being then present. The young Man was dismist, and she was bidden by the Court not to tell lyes; and was improved (after as she had been before) to give Evidence against the Prisoners.

At Execution, Mr. Noyes urged Sarah Good to Confess, and told her she was a Witch, and she knew she was a Witch, to which she replied, "you are a lyer; I am no more a Witch than you are a Wizard, and if you take away my Life, God will give you Blood to drink."

CHAPTER TWO

Peace Movements in Colonial America

The Quakers were the largest and most successful group of religious outsiders in colonial America. Formally identified today as the Religious Society of Friends, these followers of the seventeeth-century Englishman George Fox—known for their commitment to peace and pacifism—became a dominant religious and cultural force in the colony of Pennsylvania and a significant presence in the adjacent colonies of New Jersey and Delaware. Their experiences as outsiders-turned-insiders who became outsiders again demonstrates the dramatic difference between the situation of outsiders and insiders. The Quaker presence in Pennsylvania created a congenial environment that attracted numerous additional religious communities, including other groups committed to peace and nonviolence.

The Friends—another name for the Quakers—embodied the central concerns of their founder George Fox. Of humble origins, Fox grew to manhood in an England wracked by both political and religious conflict. The English civil war that broke out in 1642 pitted Parliament and the king against each other, and the Puritan movement against the state-supported Church of England. In this context Fox abandoned his apprenticeship as a shoemaker, as well as his family and friends, and set out on a pilgrimage, seeking truth and enlightenment.

The apparent gap between Christian profession and practice was especially bothersome to Fox. The suffering caused by warfare troubled him deeply. At times he experienced periods of spiritual depression. On one occasion Fox wrote:

> Now during the time that I was at Barnet [a town in Hertfordshire, England] a strong temptation to despair came upon me. And then I saw how Christ was tempted, and mighty troubles I was in. And sometimes I kept myself retired in my chamber, and often walked solitary in the Chase [the lane] there, to wait upon the Lord.... But temptations grew more and more, and I was tempted almost to despair, and when Satan could not effect his design upon me that way, then he laid snares for me and baits to draw me to commit some sin, whereby he might take advantage to bring me to despair.

After several years of turmoil, searching, and travel, George Fox found peace in the conviction that each person has access to the Inner Light of Christ. If individuals will follow that light or leading, they will find truth and perfection. This inner principle—also called the Divine Light and the Seed of God—was an illuminating, saving reality for him. Fox viewed it as a transforming presence with radical implications for his life and activities.

Fox's spiritual realization concerning the Inner Light empowered and emboldened him. He stopped taking part in conventional religious activities, such as attending church. In 1647 he began to preach openly about the idea of Christ Within. His proclamation produced a negative backlash, and as early as 1649 he was imprisoned because of his religious activities. But that opposition did not deter Fox from proclaiming his views wherever he could find an audience, whether that was in the fields, inside churches, at inns, or while on his travels. In Fox's *Journal*, published after his death, he recorded the details of his life. In it he repeatedly takes note that the power of the Lord came upon him, and then he was compelled to proclaim his message and to preach regardless of his circumstances.

Fox's moral earnestness and his willingness to suffer persecution for the sake of the truth soon won him followers whom he organized under the name of Friends of the Truth. He and his disciples gained notoriety for their unconventional, indeed somewhat eccentric, behavior. Fox, for example, often went into established churches during worship services and intentionally disturbed the proceedings, arguing with the ministers or priests. Like the Hebrew prophets in the Bible, he challenged their authority and ridiculed them publicly. On one occasion in Nottingham, when the "mighty power" of God came upon him, Fox entered a church and denounced the priest in the pulpit, whom he described in his *Journal* as resembling "a great lump of earth." He then lectured the congregation on the error of their religious "opinions." He was promptly arrested by local officials and thrown into prison. Prisons in seventeenth-century England were very undesirable places. Fox described the jail in Nottingham as "a pitiful, stinking place, where the wind brought all the stench of the house of office [the outhouse] in the place, where the stench of the place was in my throat and head many days after."

Fox expected opposition, harassment, and persecution. In fact, he seemed to relish it. On one occasion in Mansfield-Woodhouse, after a priest had finished a service, Fox "declared the Truth" to those who were assembled in the church. "But the people fell upon me," he wrote, "with their fists, books, and without compassion or mercy beat me down in the steeple-house and almost smothered me in it, being under them." They shoved him against the walls and then threw him out of the building. He was "sorely bruised and beat." Subsequently, they set him in the stocks, a wooden device that confined him, and pelted him with stones. Later they threatened him with pistols and told him that if he ever came again they would kill him. Fox regarded such suffering as part of his religious calling. He closed his account of this incident in his *Journal* as follows: "I was so bruised that I could not turn in my bed, and bruised inwardly at my heart, but after a while the power of the Lord went through me and healed me, that I was well, glory be to the Lord for ever."

Fox and the Quakers drew several radical religious conclusions from the principle of the Inner Light. He rejected, for example, the notion widely held by many religious groups at the time, including the Puritans in England and the colonies, that individuals were inherently sinful and corrupt. On the contrary, he emphasized the positive qualities of humans, including the possibility of perfection. Fox did not agree with the idea that the Bible contained all necessary religious truth. Rather, he said, each person must listen to the voice of Christ Within and follow that leading. He was unwilling to place responsibility for salvation exclusively on the crucifixion of Jesus Christ. Instead he emphasized the role of Christ as a model of the perfect life, as a person who had listened to the Voice Within.

This inner spiritual principle became the reason that the Quakers abandoned many traditional religious practices. They criticized the ceremonies and rituals that were customary to Christian worship, arguing that authentic Christianity did not require such rites. True worship involved the cultivation of the inner being. Fox rejected the Christian sacraments of baptism and the Lord's Supper (the Eucharist, or Holy Communion) because both involved material entities. In baptism, a rite of initiation, water symbolically cleanses the individual entering the church; in Communion, a sacramental meal, participants consume bread and wine associated with Christ's body and blood. Fox declared such physical elements unnecessary for true worship. The Quakers also rejected the use of other traditional worship aids, including candles, incense, and statues.

Similarly, the Friends under Fox's leadership abandoned the notion that worship should be led by ministers or priests who had special insight or knowledge about God. They denounced such leaders as "hirelings" and rejected the idea of a paid clergy. After all, they declared, everyone has equal access to spiritual insight through the Light Within. Therefore Quaker meetings did not center on either the sacraments or a sermon. When Friends gathered for worship, they met in silence, waiting for the leading of Christ Within. When that spirit spoke to someone, that individual rose to address the assembly. Men, women, and children—all might address the meeting when prompted by the Inner Light.

The Quakers assembled in meetinghouses, or buildings that lacked the traditional architectural and structural features of Christian churches, such as altars, pulpits, stained-glass windows, statues, organs, crosses, or steeples. Fox denounced the church buildings of his day as "idolatrous temples" and "steeplehouses." The plain meetinghouse physically reflected the spirit of the Friends.

This principle of plainness was also evident in the lifestyle adopted by Fox and his followers. They sought to live in a manner consistent with their understanding of the voice of Christ Within. They looked to the example provided by Jesus, who did not dwell with the rich and powerful but rather the common folk. The Quakers called for Christians to adopt a plain and modest style in both clothing and conversation.

The Inner Light prohibited Friends from engaging in any kind of violence against other people. The suffering caused by the English civil war deeply repulsed Fox, and his hostility to violence was one result. Even when attacked or physically abused, the Quakers did not defend themselves, but rather chose to suffer in the name of their religious principles. Pacifism has marked the Quaker tradition from its beginnings.

Fox's immense spiritual energy and charismatic behavior attracted many to this movement and set off a burst of controversial activity among his followers. The early Quakers acquired notoriety for their radical actions. Some invaded church buildings with blackened faces, standing silently in condemnation of those attending worship. Some stood in the streets with yokes on their necks, testifying against the corruptions of the day. A few followed the example of the prophet Isaiah, walking about naked in order to call attention to their testimony. No wonder Quakers were frequently arrested and placed in prison. These actions had the tactical advantage of drawing attention to the movement. But, simultaneously, they had the disadvantage of discrediting the movement in the eyes of those who did not share the Friends' views.

Perhaps the most notorious outburst of prophetic activity occurred in October 1656, when James Nayler, one of Fox's most prominent followers, rode into the city of Bristol, England, on a donkey in imitation of Jesus' entry into Jerusalem on Palm Sunday. Those who accompanied him shouted hosannas, or exclamations of praise and adoration. Nayler's actions, regarded by authorities as both offensive and blasphemous, led to his arrest, trial, and punishment.

These circumstances and the recognition that a charismatic, or spirit-filled, movement might self-destruct without strong leadership and a measure of discipline led Fox to begin organizing the young movement. He drew up rules for the conduct of the meetings that prescribed certain behavior and censured other activity. He undertook a series of missionary journeys to locations where scattered Quakers had settled. At these sites he used his personal influence to organize his followers. He appointed elders and overseers to supervise the meetings. In 1671–72 Fox's travels brought him to America, where he visited with Friends and promoted the growth of the movement in the New World. He was a tireless advocate of the cause of truth and a skillful organizer.

But Fox was not the person primarily responsible for the Quaker presence in America. That was the accomplishment of William Penn, the son of an English admiral and an acquaintance of King James II. Already, as an undergraduate at Oxford University, Penn refused to conform to the practices of the Church of England. By 1667 he had accepted the Quaker way of life and shortly afterward began to write in defense of Quaker principles. His publication entitled *The Sandy Foundation Shaken* (1668) gave voice to his unorthodox views on the doctrine of the

Trinity comprising the Father, Son, and Holy Spirit, and on the doctrine of the atonement or the redeeming work of Christ; ultimately this publication led to his imprisonment in the Tower of London. While in prison he wrote *No Cross, No Crown* (1669), which was a celebration of a willingness to endure persecution for the sake of truth. A jury later acquitted him of the charge of unitarianism, a view that explicitly rejected the orthodox notion of the Trinity.

Penn emerged as a leading advocate of religious toleration. He became interested in founding a colony in America, where liberty of conscience might be guaranteed. In 1681 he obtained a charter from the king, in partial payment of a debt owed to his father, for land in the New World, a land grant that ultimately became the colony of Pennsylvania. Penn arrived in America in October 1682 after nine weeks at sea on a voyage that saw some thirty passengers die of smallpox. Before leaving England he had written a publication designed to attract settlers to the new colony. It contrasted the conditions in England with more favorable prospects, both economic and political, in the New World and promised religious toleration of all who came. He also advertised for settlers in those parts of continental Europe to which he had previously traveled.

Penn was the governor of the colony, owned the land, and was responsible for establishing its constitution and laws. He authored its Frame of Government in 1682—a document favoring the proprietor—which he later revised to give greater power to the popular assembly. Before the year was out a stream of settlers came to Pennsylvania, eventually including Friends from all parts of the British Isles as well as religious groups from the Rhine country in Germany. Penn returned to England in 1684 and carried out much of his administration of the colony through deputy governors and as an absentee landlord, a decision that led to considerable criticism. He returned to America for a second stay in Pennsylvania from 1699 to 1701, but the colony was never his long-term residence.

Penn's religious interests, however, had a direct impact on his American colony. In 1696 he wrote a defense of Quaker doctrine and practice entitled *Primitive Christianity Revived, in the Faith and Practice of the People Called Quakers.* Starting with the fundamental principle "That God, through Christ, hath placed a Principle in every Man, to inform him of his Duty, and to enable him to do it," Penn spelled out a variety of conclusions to be drawn by Quakers. He condemned tithes, or obligatory payments to support ministers; swearing, or the taking of oaths; marriages between Quakers and those from outside the community; recreation and pastimes associated with the world; holy days, whether they be fasts or feasts; all signs of worldly honor, such as the use of "Modish Salutations of the Times" including formal titles; and all war among Christians. Penn called for plainness of speech, plainness in apparel and furniture, moderation in food, and concern for the poor.

The Quakers who came to America under Penn's leadership were not the first Friends in the English colonies. Nor were they the first to establish the regular series of meetings among Quakers. George Fox's organizational scheme took hold in the New World. The first local meeting in America was probably organized in 1670; subsequently the Friends set up a monthly meeting in 1678, followed by the quarterly and yearly meetings in 1680 and 1681, respectively. These provided religious structure for the large number of Quakers who poured into the Pennsylvania area. By 1700 more than forty local meetings were organized in Pennsylvania.

These regular meetings became the method of governance within the Society of Friends. Among the actions taken by the early Quaker meetings in America were disciplinary steps against Friends who passed counterfeit money, who gave liquor to the Indians, and who bought stolen property from them. The meetings also censured one person for "extravagant powdering" of his wig. Quaker meetings attempted to enforce appropriate standards of behavior within the community.

The Quakers quickly emerged as the leading political faction in the colony of Pennsylvania. Penn intended to create a haven for the Friends and other groups who were persecuted, and he succeeded beyond his own expectations. The attractiveness of the colony and its positive economic prospects drew non-Quakers to the region. Yet Friends formed the largest portion of the population, and therefore Quakers were the controlling party in the Pennsylvania assembly in Philadelphia. With Penn as the proprietor of the colony and with an elected Quaker majority in the colonial assembly, the Friends had gone from the situation of persecuted outsiders in England to the position of being the party of insiders in Pennsylvania, firmly in control of the political situation.

It is not always easy to make the transition from being an outsider to being an insider. In the case of Pennsylvania's Quakers, one difficulty related to the political responsibility of defending the colony's borders against attack by French forces allied with Native Americans. William Penn had insisted on cordial relations with the Indians, and tradition tells of his negotiating with them for the land that he had been given by the king. But the outbreak of the French and Indian Wars left the colonial frontier in a vulnerable state. The Quakers in the assembly were responsible for military affairs. That posed a major moral and political dilemma for the American Friends, who shared George Fox's commitment to pacifism. The problem reached the breaking point in the 1740s, when a large number of Quaker members withdrew from the assembly, in effect acknowledging their inability as Friends to legislate on military matters. This is an instance of the religious perspective of outsiders making life as insiders difficult. In this case the Quakers stepped away from their political responsibilities as insiders, preferring the role of outsiders.

It needs to be pointed out that the Friends were not always friendly, even with other Friends; that is, controversy can occur in a religious community committed to peace and nonviolence. In early Pennsylvania the most notable example of religious conflict involved the views of George Keith, a prominent convert to the society. Keith, a native of Scotland, became a Friend and traveled extensively with both Fox and Penn. He too was imprisoned on several occasions as a result of his bold preaching. In 1684 he emigrated to America, where he assisted with the organization of the colony of East Jersey. In America he came into conflict with the Philadelphia Yearly Meeting. Keith criticized those belonging to that meeting for placing too much emphasis on the Inner Light and paying insufficient attention to the historic Jesus. He attracted followers to his views and organized them into a society called Christian Friends. The Philadelphia Quaker meeting disowned him, and he returned to England in 1693. Keith eventually became affiliated with the Church of England, was ordained to the Anglican priesthood, and in 1702 returned to America for a two-year period as a missionary and agent of the Society for the Propagation of the Gospel.

By the middle of the eighteenth century Quakerism had changed a great deal. The worldview and spiritual values of the Friends had been shaped initially by their radical dissent from the religious and social patterns of mid-seventeenth-century England. The outsider mentality was not easily set aside. But prophetic protest was no longer appropriate in America once the Quakers found themselves the dominant political and religious faction in Pennsylvania. Prosperity, which came quickly in the New World, also presented a challenge to the plain lifestyle. Friends now could afford the finer things of life. Change was inevitable in these circumstances.

Pennsylvania quickly became attractive to other religious groups in Europe that were experiencing hardship and persecution. The moderate climate, abundant land for farming, tolerant political environment, favorable economic prospects, plus William Penn's systematic efforts to recruit settlers, attracted a growing stream of immigrants to Pennsylvania. They brought with them a variety of alternative religions. Two of them shared with the Quakers a strong commitment to pacifism.

These were the Mennonites and the Amish, both offshoots of the Anabaptist (a word meaning to "rebaptize") wing, or the most radical branch of the Protestant Reformation in Europe. The two sects, while related in significant ways, developed their own organizations and institutions. Eventually both prospered in Pennsylvania.

The Mennonites, the larger of the two, took their name from their founder Menno Simons, a parish priest in Freisland, the Netherlands, who renounced the Catholic Church in 1536 and joined the radical Anabaptist movement. He spent the remaining twenty–five years of his life organizing and nurturing groups of Anabaptists in the Netherlands and surrounding territories.

These were extremely difficult times for the Anabaptists, who were persecuted and harassed throughout Europe.

Menno Simons' religious views reflected a sectarian mentality. He believed that Christians ought to reform the church by following closely the pattern of first-century believers described in the New Testament. He rejected the practice of infant baptism, reserving that sacrament for adults who could acknowledge their beliefs. Simons emphasized the authority of local fellowships rather than that exercised through highly structured bureaucratic organizations, such as those in the Roman Catholic and many Protestant churches. He called for the separation of church and state and rejected any involvement of Christians in the leadership of the civil government. He also affirmed the principle of pacifism and nonviolence. As a result of the latter, the Mennonites often resorted to migration throughout Europe in response to opposition against them.

The first group of Mennonites to migrate to America came in 1683 and settled in Germantown. They hailed from Krefeld on the Lower Rhine. They were attracted to Pennsylvania by a grant of 18,000 acres. During the years immediately following, a limited number of additional Mennonites came to Pennsylvania, most of whom spoke German. After 1710 these numbers were augmented by a more sizable influx of Mennonites of Swiss extraction. The new settlers expanded into the areas west of Germantown, which was near Philadelphia, eventually concentrating their settlements in what became Lancaster County in Pennsylvania. Yet it was in Germantown that the first formal congregation of Mennonites was formed. For the initial twenty–five years in America, Mennonite religious activities had been unstructured and without the services of regular clergy. In this situation Mennonite families often joined other churches or worshiped with other sects. In the spring of 1708 that changed, for in that month Jacob Godschalk, a newly designated bishop, administered the first sacrament service among Mennonites in the New World. A few weeks earlier he had baptized eleven adults. Four years later the adult membership of that congregation included ninety-nine baptized adults.

The Amish, another small Anabaptist sect that found Pennsylvania congenial, originated as a conservative faction within the Swiss Brethren, a Protestant group that was also part of the Radical or Anabaptist Reformation. The Amish took their name from the leader of their group, Jakob Ammann, an elder in a community located in the canton, or district, of Berne, Switzerland. Ammann differed from his coreligionists on a number of issues. In most cases he opted for the more conservative position.

Ammann called for strict observance of several practices. He wanted to administer the Lord's Supper more frequently than the Swiss Brethren did and to retain the practice of foot washing in the Communion service as a sign of humility, a ceremony based on the New Testament account of Jesus' washing the feet of his disciples. He insisted that the members of his community wear plain clothing and avoid all signs of ostentation or worldliness. He required that the men retain untrimmed beards. Finally, and most importantly, Ammann demanded the total shunning, or ban, of those who were excommunicated from the fellowship. That is, he insisted that there be no interaction with those who abandoned the faith, even if they were members of one's family.

Ammann had the most success in attracting converts to his movement in the areas of southern Germany and Alsace. His followers began to migrate to America in the early decades of the eighteenth century. Their earliest settlements were in the region of Berks and Lancaster Counties in Pennsylvania, areas in which Mennonite families were already present. Eventually the Amish would join with others in the area and push farther to the west. It is estimated that by the end of the colonial era some seventy Amish congregations existed in the colony. There were no Amish church buildings, though, because they held their worship services in the homes of families in the congregation.

The Mennonites and the Amish were linked religiously in many ways, despite their different historical backgrounds. Both carried forward the sectarian orientation of the Anabaptist Reformation, dissenting from the religious patterns of the Roman Catholic Church and the major Protestant communities. Both groups, as a point of pride, retained ancestral customs. Both regarded the Bible as the source of their religious authority. They strongly emphasized the principle of obedience as a measure of the Christian life. Therefore violations of the regulations of the community were dealt with severely. Religious leaders were chosen by the community and were called bishops. Both communities drew sharp boundaries around themselves and attempted to maintain their group identity by avoiding involvement with those outside the community. Intermarriage with outsiders was forbidden. Both groups urged their members to live simply, avoiding luxury.

The Mennonites and the Amish strongly affirmed the principle of nonresistance: They were unwilling to take oaths, to support capital punishment or execution for crimes, or to take part in warfare. In these respects they were allied with their Quaker neighbors in Pennsylvania, each group testifying to its understanding of the truth.

The colony of Pennsylvania became a haven for Friends, Mennonites, Amish, and a host of other small dissenting religious groups that found themselves harassed and persecuted elsewhere. In Pennsylvania dissenters found a home among other dissenters.

Europe in the seventeenth century was an increasingly hostile place for many religious dissenters. For that reason William Penn found highly receptive audiences on the Continent, where he recruited settlers for his colony in America. Written from southern Germany to his son Henry in Pennsylvania, Heinrich Frey's letter reveals the reasons that Mennonites and others were drawn to Pennsylvania and the excitement they felt anticipating immigration to America.

Heilbron, February 6, 1681

Dear Son:

Your letter from faraway America reached us by the hand of the brave Captain Souder and gave us great joy, and when a few days later the father of your true friend came to see us our joy knew no bounds.

America, according to your writing, must be a beautiful land. We rejoice greatly that your home is with such good God-fearing people, and that the Indians in your community are a peace-loving people.

Dear Henry, since you have been away from us conditions in south Germany have become very much worse. The French have wrought much devastation, and this is pressing us very hard at this time, and besides we now suffer from the plague of high taxes.

Thousands would gladly leave the Fatherland if they

had the means to do so. A merchant from Frankfurt was with us last week and informed us how along the Rhine a number of families have banded together to accept the invitation of an Englishman, named William Penn, who had recently visited that community, to settle in that beautiful land and there establish new homes. After I had received this information I went at once to our minister, whose parents live at Worms, on the Rhine, and begged him earnestly to learn what truth there was in these reports and to find out, if possible, if there would be any opportunity for us to join them and go to the New World. He then informed me that these reports were all true and that he had been informed by one who had inside knowledge, that in a place called Kriegsheim, near Worms, many were preparing themselves to go to the New World. When I gave the good man your letter to read, he was greatly surprised, and said that you were on the land to which these emigrants are going. It is the good providence of God that has shown these burdened people so glorious a land. We, as also the Plattenbach family, are only waiting for a good opportunity when the dear Lord will bring us to you.

Your brother Peter is learning shoemaking and will soon be free. America is the only dream of Elizabeth. Catharine, only six years old, asks us daily, "Will we soon be going to our brother in America?"

Your dear mother, as also your brother and sisters, greet you heartily and pray to the dear Lord that he may protect and ever keep you.

From your loving father,

Heinrich Frey.

CHAPTER THREE

Communitarians Living on the Margins

V iolence against people trying to live according to their religious beliefs was commonplace in the United States during the nineteenth century. One striking example occurred in 1825 at a village called Pleasant Hill in central Kentucky. This site was home to several hundred Shakers, members of a religious community founded by Ann Lee, an eighteenth-century English prophet. In early June the village was attacked by a mob organized by family members of Lucy Bryant, a teenage girl who had joined the community. Lucy's relatives were intent on forcing her to leave the Shakers because they believed she was being held against her will, which was not the case.

On the evening of June 6 a group of forty to fifty men, "armed with clubs, dirks [short daggers], or pistols" broke into the Shakers' central dwelling and randomly assaulted them. "The clubbing went on furiously considerable time," the Shaker elders reported, "till a number of Brethren and Sisters were inhumanly beaten, some of which were knocked Sensless." Eventually the mob was persuaded to leave after speaking directly with Lucy Bryant, who was determined to stay.

One week later a larger mob, several hundred in number, described as "savage looking," reappeared at the village, led this time by Lucy Bryant's mother, who resembled "a fury from the lower regions." This time the mob dragged Lucy off despite her protests. The Shakers were unable to stop this assault because, like the Quakers, Mennonites, and Amish, they too were committed to pacifism and nonviolence.

The challenge of living according to one's beliefs faces religious people everywhere and in every age. That challenge was especially great for religious communitarians—people motivated to live in communities apart from the rest of society—who held social views that were often unconventional, controversial, and unpopular. A number of such outsider groups rose to prominence in the early years of the new American republic.

The First Amendment to the Constitution of the United States, adopted in 1791, guarantees the free exercise of religion. That guarantee had the practical effect of encouraging and protecting radical religious and social innovation among communities on the margins, behavior that often went against prevailing patterns.

Among the markers commonly setting these outsiders apart from the rest of American society were four distinguishing actions. Religious communitarians typically separated themselves physically from those who did not accept the same beliefs. They withdrew from contact and formed distinct villages or settlements whenever possible. Second, the members of these communities typically established an independent economic base for their societies by pooling their resources and holding their assets in common rather than in private. This financial arrangement can be called a form of communism because in theory the community as a whole rather than individuals owned all property; the communitarians shared their goods, distributing resources to individuals according to their needs. Third, communitarians often lived outside the conventional family structure, consisting of husband, wife, children, and grandparents. In its place they experimented with different arrangements, sometimes defining these relationships as a new kind of family. Finally, these outsiders occasionally went further and redefined the function of sexual relations within the new social order. Some groups prohibited all sexual activity; other communities extended the circle of those who were permitted to engage in sexual relations.

Because of these innovations, religious communitarians were the frequent object of criticism, ridicule, harassment, and physical attack. That pattern of hostility was especially true in the early decades of the new American nation, despite the constitutional guarantee of religious freedom.

The most successful communitarians in the early nineteenth century were the Shakers. Their founder, Ann Lee, was an uneducated, simple, working-class woman. Lee emerged as a religious visionary and prophet after she joined a small group of sectarians in Manchester, England, known by the name of Shaking Quakers. The sect was not part of the organized Society of Friends, or Quakers. They were called Shaking Quakers, or Shakers, because they shook or trembled when possessed by the spirit of God or when they engaged in ecstatic or trancelike activity.

The Shakers attracted public attention in England when they openly challenged the established church. Members of the sect invaded Anglican worship services and disturbed the proceedings in an effort to gain attention for their ideas. Lee, members of her family, and other Believers (as the Shakers called themselves) were confident that their cause was righteous. Their actions, not surprisingly, resulted in arrest and imprisonment. On more than one occasion Lee was jailed as a result of her protests aimed at the churches.

The negative response to the Shakers was one reason that Lee, her husband, who was a blacksmith, and a handful of followers left England in 1774 and traveled to America, arriving on August 6 at the port of New York. Another reason for the journey, according to Shaker tradition, was that Lee had a vision instructing her to carry her message to the New World. The Shakers disappeared from historical view for several years after their arrival. Their public story resumes near the end of the decade, by which time they had settled together—minus Lee's husband—in an area near Albany, New York, known as Niskeyuna.

These were the years of the American Revolution, and the small band of English Shakers attracted suspicion during that conflict because it was thought that they might be British sympathizers. At one point in 1780 colonial authorities arrested Lee and several followers and charged them with attempting to supply nearby English military forces with food. The charges—though false—seemed reasonable to many because the Shakers refused to bear arms on behalf of the American cause. The Believers were pacifists and would not use force against anyone, not even in self-defense. Ann Lee spent more than four months in prison before being released on bail on the condition that she maintain "good Behavior" and not do anything to harm the patriot cause.

That same year—1780—witnessed the beginning of Shaker religious successes among their neighbors in eastern New York and nearby western Massachusetts. Protestants in the region, especially members of Separate Baptist churches, heard about this group of "strange and wonderful Christians," to use the description of Valentine Rathbun, an early convert. They lived near the Hudson River and worshiped in unusual ways. Their leader, who was called Mother, demanded much of her followers. Some of the curious visited Niskeyuna, and they reported that the Shakers worshiped by whirling and dancing in ecstasy. Ann Lee—Mother—testified harshly against sins of the flesh and worked wonders, according to her followers. She declared the path of righteousness to be the way of the cross, that is, sacrifice or denial of the practices of the world. Lee prophesied powerfully and with great urgency against the churches and prevailing social patterns. She and her faithful English followers soon attracted a steady stream of American converts who accepted the Shaker challenge to live a more strenuous Christian life.

Beginning in May 1781 Lee and her closest associates left Niskeyuna and began traveling through parts of eastern New York and New England, visiting sites where converts resided and seeking to persuade others to accept the Shaker life. Massachusetts was the principal scene of their activities, but they also spent time in Rhode Island and Connecticut. The purpose of the journey was to strengthen and encourage new converts in their faith and to testify to the Shaker gospel among the world's people. The Believers held public meetings in which they declared that redemption was possible only within their society. They demanded that Believers abandon "natural generation," their term for sexual relations, and confess their sins to one of the leaders in the community. Lee also spoke about the possibility of perfection for those who denied the flesh and pursued holiness.

The results of this prolonged missionary journey were mixed. On the one hand, the band of traveling Shakers enjoyed considerable success in winning new converts. They were especially successful in Harvard, Massachusetts, where they converted several former members of a celibate community that had been founded by Shadrach Ireland, a charismatic, or spirit-filled, Baptist preacher. On the other hand, the Believers also aroused immense hostility in a number of locations. Lee was the special target of the animosity. She was repeatedly accused of being a witch and a man. She experienced physical persecution, as did others traveling with her who were whipped, stoned, and forced to flee for their safety. Violence was one of the reasons that the Shakers returned to Niskeyuna in September 1783 after twenty-eight months on the road.

The long missionary journey was the high point of Lee's public ministry. In 1784, less than a year after her return to Niskeyuna, she was dead. Her followers attributed her death to the hostility and persecution she had experienced. The Believers praised her as the Elect Lady of the Bible. Some Shakers spoke of her as the second Christ. Her enemies depicted her as a violent and deceptive woman, a person given to drunkenness and promiscuity.

Following Lee's death, leadership in the young community fell on the shoulders of her fervent English disciple James Whittaker.

Three years later, when he died, two prominent American converts, Joseph Meacham and Lucy Wright, took on the responsibilities of leadership associated with the Central Ministry of the expanding community. During the next three decades they led the efforts to build a national communitarian society.

In the years after Lee's death, the Believers gathered in villages set apart from the world. Elders and eldresses appointed by the Central Ministry presided over each of the settlements. Converts to Shakerism were required to confess their sins and forsake the world of the flesh. Believers consecrated their possessions, whether money, real estate, or movable goods, to the Shaker cause. In doing so, they abandoned the principle of private property. They also agreed to work for the common good. One of Lee's most cherished sayings was "Hands to work, and hearts to God." The Believers constituted themselves a spiritual family with the elders and eldresses functioning as their parents, making all men and women brothers and sisters. Lee's assault on the flesh became a community commitment to celibacy—that is, abstinence from all sexual activity.

By the second decade of the nineteenth century the Believers had expanded from their initial location outside Albany, throughout New England, and into the Ohio Valley. In 1805 Lucy Wright had dispatched three Shaker missionaries to the new territories west of the Allegheny Mountains, where they succeeded in attracting converts in Ohio and Kentucky. Many who joined the community came from the ranks of the Baptists, Methodists, and Presbyterians. By 1823 there were eighteen Shaker villages, stretching from Maine in the East to Indiana and Kentucky in the West. Two decades later there were nearly forty-five hundred members of the United Society of Believers in Christ's Second Appearing, the formal name of the national organization.

Rising economic success accompanied the geographical and numerical expansion of the Shakers. Despite condemnation of the ways of the world and the strategy of withdrawal from it, the Shakers prospered, even when measured by worldly standards. Their collective work ethic was one factor contributing to that success. They also were enterprising and innovative in both agriculture and commerce. They gained a reputation for honesty and for high-quality products—whether seeds, brooms, chairs, or patent medicines. Visitors to their villages usually praised the Shakers.

At the same time, however, the Shakers continued to be assaulted by critics who charged them with erroneous beliefs and criminal practices. Opponents accused them of elevating Ann Lee to the stature of Christ, of breaking apart families, of holding members against their will, and of duping converts out of their financial resources. They alleged that Shaker leaders abused their authority and used the community's assets for their own personal gain. Believers frequently were the object of hostile lawsuits and as a result spent a considerable amount of time defending the religious beliefs and social practices of the society.

In the years after the Civil War the United Society of Believers experienced a steady numerical decline in their villages and a geographical retreat to the East Coast. The Shakers failed to retain as adult members the children that they often cared for in their settlements; they also attracted fewer and fewer males to the community. Villages were forced to close because the remaining Believers were not able to sustain themselves economically. Among some, the commitment to the Shaker way of life and to the community's values waned. Aging women made up the majority of the remaining society by the middle of the twentieth century, confined at that point to three remaining villages located in New England. At the start of the twenty-first century a single village remains at Sabbathday Lake, Maine, carrying on the tradition with a handful of Believers.

Throughout their history, the Shakers have represented a clear alternative to a number of widely accepted American values. They rejected private property, the traditional family unit, the positive function of sexual intercourse, the principle of democratic government, and the notion of patriarchal, or male, dominance. They shared their possessions, created a new extended, nonbiological spiritual family, rejected all sexual activity, accepted the authority of the ministry, and gave women new levels of responsibility in their community. These positions were genuinely radical in the first half of the nineteenth century. These views and practices are still at odds with the values held by most Americans.

The United States attracted other charismatic and prophetic figures inclined toward communitarianism. George Rapp, a weaver and religious dissident from Württemberg, Germany, is a notable example. He emerged on the public scene in Germany as a vigorous critic of the Lutheran Church, denouncing its theology and worship services as cold and lifeless. He turned to the study of the Bible and to a more emotional approach to religion. When he began gathering others who shared his judgments, Rapp encountered opposition from local authorities, both religious and civil. His separatist views also included resistance to military service. He was briefly imprisoned, and his followers were repeatedly harassed.

But this official opposition had the opposite effect from what was intended. Rapp grew more confident in his view that God had chosen him to lead the group. In 1803, as pressures mounted on his community, Rapp sailed for the United States, hoping to find a location where he and his disciples might settle and take advantage of religious freedom under the Constitution. He purchased five thousand acres north of Pittsburgh, and the following year three hundred German followers came to the United States. During their first year, many scattered throughout nearby states, working for other farmers to produce income. Rapp and some of the men cleared the land and built houses. In 1805 the community gathered at the site they named Harmony and organized themselves into the Harmony Society, numbering some seven hundred and fifty men, women, and children.

At this point the Harmonists adopted a form of communitarian living. They placed their assets into a common fund and gave to the members as they had need. By the end of their first year of communal living, the village included more than fifty houses, a church, a school, and a gristmill. The Harmonists were accustomed to hard work, and their efforts soon brought a modest measure of economic success to the community through agriculture and the production of lumber, hides, wool, and whiskey.

The first decade in the United States brought additional important changes to this community. Rapp continued intensive study of the Bible, and on the basis of the book of Revelation became convinced that the promise given to the church of Philadelphia in Rev. 3:8–12 applied to his community, that they would be given "the name of the city of my god, which is new Jerusalem." He believed that if the Harmonists persisted in the face of temptation, denied themselves, and endured persecution, they would reign with Christ when he returned to earth. This belief was an exalted view of the community's importance. Additionally, Rapp thought that since the Bible described the faithful as virgins, the members of the community ought to imitate Christ and be celibate. Therefore in 1807, at his insistence, the community adopted the practice of celibacy. Unlike the Shakers, who separated men and women physically, however, the Harmonists allowed families to remain together and simply called for an end to sexual relations. This development is evidence of the dominant role that George Rapp—Father Rapp, as he was called—played in the life of the community. He exercised control over all aspects of religious and social affairs. In this leadership role his adopted son Friedrich assisted him.

The Harmonists, or Rappites, did not remain long in Pennsylvania. In 1814 the community moved to a new site of thirty thousand acres in southwestern Indiana adjacent to the Wabash River. They sold their Pennsylvania location for $100,000. In Indiana the group again set to work, clearing the land and building a village. They left their first location because it lacked waterways to markets for their goods and because they wanted to cultivate grapes, which required a different environment. In Indiana they were greeted with suspicion by their neighbors, in part because they persisted in the use of the German language. They also experienced repeated bouts of malaria. And yet again the Harmonists quickly achieved a measure of economic success.

After ten years the Harmony Society moved once again, this time back to western Pennsylvania, to a location on the Ohio River they named Economy. They sold the village in Indiana for $150,000 to Robert Owen, a Scottish reformer, who established his own community of New Harmony at the site. The society again enjoyed economic prosperity, and yet developments during the following years were not all favorable. Conflict broke out within the community over Rapp's leadership and over some of the demands he made on the Harmonists. In 1832 a large group, estimated at one third of the community, joined Bernard Muller, who called himself Count Leon, and defected. Muller rejected Rapp's leadership, favored reintroduction of marriage, and argued for ending some of the prohibitions requisite to the simple lifestyle of the Harmonists. Despite this major defection and the subsequent death of his son Friedrich in 1834, in his last years Rapp remained confident that he had been chosen to deliver his virgin community to Christ in person upon his return to earth. He died confident of that role. The community numbered more than a thousand members at the time of his death.

While the Harmonists experienced steady numerical decline in the years after the Civil War, they enjoyed expanding economic prosperity. But poor leadership in the closing decade of the nineteenth century resulted in the loss of the community's fortune. The society was formally dissolved in 1905, and more than a decade later its assets were taken over by the state of Pennsylvania.

Brook Farm, though very short-lived, was perhaps the most celebrated communitarian effort in American history. It achieved that status because of the prominent people who participated in it and wrote about it, including author Nathaniel Hawthorne. George Ripley, the Harvard-trained minister of the Unitarian Purchase Street Church in Boston, founded Brook Farm in 1841 at West Roxbury, Massachusetts. Earlier he had been a driving force in the formation of the Transcendental Club, as well as in plans for publication of *The Dial*, both institutional expressions of transcendentalism, a broad-ranging intellectual movement with religious implications. Transcendentalists rejected the institutional religion of their day and asserted very positive views of human possibility. Ripley, by disposition and training a man of letters, became the first president of Brook Farm at a point when its formal title was The Brook-Farm Association for Industry and Education. It began as a cooperative residential community organized as a joint-stock venture intent on ensuring a "more natural union" between the thinker and the worker. It placed the highest value on mental freedom and attracted a distinguished group of "liberal, intelligent, and cultivated persons," including Ralph Waldo Emerson and Henry David Thoreau, which in fact proved to be a major part of the problems that developed almost immediately. Intellectual discussion flourished among the young who joined the venture, but both the farming and the work of artisans within the community lagged. In an effort to improve productivity and increase membership, in 1844 the community converted formally to the principles of the Frenchman Charles Fourier, who had called for the establishment of planned communities called phalanxes in which cooperation would replace competition. Fourier's theory called for an ideal community in which members lived together in a central dwelling with detailed organization of all aspects of activity.

Brook Farm quickly became the hub of the Fourierist movement in the United States and a positive influence for the cause of cooperation. Unfortunately, a fire destroyed the new phalanstery—the name given to the community's central dwelling—and that disaster brought an effective end to the Brook Farm experiment.

The contrast with both the Shakers and Harmonists could not be greater. Brook Farm was premised on liberal religious and intellectual ideas; its members valued individual freedom most highly. Intellectuals prospered, but there were too few laborers. Indulgence, not self-denial, was the rule at Brook Farm. Freedom, concern with self, and individual creative expression failed to provide the solid foundation necessary for Brook Farm to succeed as a communitarian effort.

Perhaps the most controversial religious communitarian group that emerged in the period before the Civil War was the Oneida Community begun by John Humphrey Noyes, a native of Brattleboro, Vermont. Unlike both Ann Lee and George Rapp, he was descended from a respected New England family and enjoyed the advantages of a middle-class economic background. He attended Dartmouth College and subsequently was trained as a minister first at Andover Theological Seminary and then at Yale Divinity School. In those years he became increasingly preoccupied with the doctrine of personal holiness or perfectionism. He struggled for several years with this idea, trying to understand God's demands for total perfection, and was frustrated by his own efforts to achieve that religious goal. During that time he experienced periods of extreme depression.

By 1837 Noyes was in Putney, Vermont, where he organized and led a Bible study group. In that context he began to speak about his increasingly radical ideas, including his views on perfectionism, and judgments concerning Christian love, which for him included sexual love. In time the Bible study group evolved into the Putney Community, a semicommunal organization comprising seven or eight families. In 1846 Noyes and his followers inaugurated a practice they called "complex marriage," an alternative to monogamous marriage, in which various men and women within the group had sexual relations with each other as an antidote to what they perceived as the selfishness of the exclusive sexual relationship between a husband and a wife. Noyes, who had married in 1838, affirmed that sexual relations were essentially good and ought to be engaged in by members of the society to foster love among them. The practice of complex marriage began with the members of the Putney Community, but when Noyes was charged by outsiders with adultery, he was forced to flee from Putney in 1847.

In 1848 Noyes and some fifty followers relocated to Oneida Creek in central New York, a region that had experienced a great deal of fervent religious activity. In this location Noyes founded the Oneida Community, which featured the principle of perfectionism as its basic religious idea. Noyes also developed other distinctive ideas, including a deep conviction that he was responsible for establishing the kingdom of God on earth. In that role he was to lead his followers in a practical demonstration of the social implications of perfection by imitating the model of the sinless Christ. Noyes thought of himself as divinely appointed to restore the knowledge of true Christianity and to usher in the final stages of history.

At Oneida Noyes carried forward his social program, inspired by what he called Bible communism, which he derived from the example of the Christian church in the first century. This economic system, based on both agriculture and manufacturing, was highly successful. Prosperity came quickly to the community. Eventually the Perfectionists built a large dwelling—the Mansion House—that accommodated several hundred residents and became the center for social, religious, and cultural activities. Noyes was dominant in all these decisions. He was a powerful leader whose authority and influence were critical at every stage of Oneida's history. Within the community he was known as Father Noyes. He wrote extensively about the social ideas on which the community stood and formulated its religious ideas and practices. One of the most distinctive processes, called mutual criticism, required a member to submit in silence to criticism from fellow Perfectionists in the hope of discovering ways to improve and move closer to holiness.

Yet it was the sexual theory and practice of Oneida that gained the most notoriety. The practice of complex marriage did not produce a steady stream of children in the community because it was accompanied by a form of male restraint in which men did not ejaculate during sexual intercourse. The practical result of this restraint was to limit the number of children born into the community and to keep the focus on what Noyes thought most important in sexual relations, the expression of love among members of the community.

From 1869 to 1879, under Noyes's direction, the community engaged in a controlled experiment designed to produce outstanding children, a practice known as eugenics. Noyes selected particular members to have offspring. The children born of these arranged sexual relationships were called stirps and the experiment *stirpiculture*, or "improvement of the race." A total of fifty-eight stirps were born during these years, nine of them fathered by Noyes himself. After birth, the stirps were cared for by committee with special concern taken for their education. Noyes was confident this was one more step toward perfection.

The Oneida Community had two small outposts in Brooklyn, New York, and Wallingford, Connecticut, where some members resided. Noyes spent a good bit of time at these locations. Yet the Oneida site was the center of this communitarian effort. Noyes was a radical thinker who defied the social and religious conventions of his day. It is no surprise that he often found himself contending with controversy, both inside and outside the community. In 1879 opposition from religious leaders in western New York mounted, and there were growing threats of legal action against Noyes because of members' unorthodox sexual arrangements. In late June, when a Syracuse newspaper ran headlines concerning the prospect of arrest, Noyes fled to Canada under the cover of darkness. He never returned to Oneida. Shortly after his departure the Perfectionists formally ended the practice of complex marriage. The following year, in 1880, the community suspended its communitarian economic practice and converted its assets into a joint-stock company, Oneida Community, Limited, a manufacturer of silver and flatware that still exists.

Communitarianism proved attractive to many nineteenth-century Americans. It offered economic cooperation, a communal work structure, shared values, brotherhood and sisterhood, and the advantages of numbers. Religious communitarians added their own particular spiritual principles that gave additional meaning to the common life. And yet success did not come easily. Hard work and sacrifice were required, as was persistence in the face of conflict and opposition.

Religious dissenters often experienced physical violence, hostility, and persecution from their opponents. Mob action against religious groups that espoused nonviolence seems offensive. While visiting her followers in Petersham, Massachusetts, in December 1781, Ann Lee and some of her close associates were the targets of violence and abusive actions recorded later by her disciples. In this account the contrast between the assault and Lee's forgiveness of her attackers is striking.

However, as the mob had withdrawn, and all danger apparently at an end, the neighboring Believers returned home, and some of the brethren, who accompanied the Elders, went with them. Those who remained were about retiring to rest, when Mother discovered, from the window, that her cruel persecutors were near, and made some attempts to conceal herself. The house was again assaulted by about thirty creatures in human shape; the doors being fastened, were burst open and broke, and these ruffians entered.

David Hammond was immediately knocked down and cruelly beaten. Mary, his woman, who had a young child in her arms, was knocked down and received severe strokes on her head, by one Thomas Carter. Elder James was clinched by the collar, knocked down and left for dead; and several others were knocked down. Father William was also hurt; and all that stood in their way were beaten and bruised more or less.

As their object was to seize Mother, the candles had been previously concealed to prevent their finding her. But this did not hinder them; they seized fire-brands and searched the house, and at length found her in a bed-room. They immediately seized her by her feet, and inhumanly dragged her, feet foremost, out of the house, and threw her into a sleigh, with as little ceremony as they would the dead carcase of a beast, and drove off, committing at the same time, acts of inhumanity and indecency which even savages would be ashamed of.

In the struggle with these inhuman wretches, she lost her cap and handkerchief, and otherwise had her clothes torn in a shameful manner. Their pretence was to find out whether she was a woman or not. In this situation, in a cold winter's night, they drove nearly three miles, to Samuel Peckham's tavern, near Petersham meeting house.

Father William, feeling great concern for Mother's safety, he and David Hammond followed the sleigh. He told the ruffians that she was his sister, and he would follow her; and attempting to hold on by the hind part of the sleigh, they gave him many blows with the butts of their sleigh-whips. He and David, however, followed them to the forementioned tavern. Elder James, being badly wounded, was not able to follow them.

It appears from information, that Samuel Peckham, who was the captain of militia, had previously agreed with the ruffians who seized Mother, to give them as much rum as they would drink, upon condition that they would bring her to his house. After their arrival, Father William and David Hammond remonstrated against the ungodliness and brutality of their behavior. David represented to them the unlawfulness of such conduct, and how they had exposed themselves to the penalties of the law.

Being, by this time ashamed of their conduct, and fearful of the consequences, they promised to release Mother, upon condition that David would sign an obligation not to prosecute them for what they had done. Being impelled by a sense of feeling for Mother's safety, he reluctantly yielded to their demands, and left them to answer at the bar of Divine Justice, concerning a species of conduct for which they were unwilling to appear before an earthly tribunal.

This being done, they released Mother, and some time in the night, some of them brought her, and those with her, back to David Hammond's. She came in, singing for joy, that she was again restored to her children. The men who brought her back, appeared to be greatly ashamed of their wicked conduct, and confessed that they had abused her shamefully, said they were sorry for it, and desired her forgiveness. Mother replied, "I can freely forgive you; I hold nothing against you, and I pray God to forgive you." So they departed peacefully.

CHAPTER FOUR

Apocalyptic Traditions: Watching and Waiting for the End

The sketch of William Miller that appeared in the *New York Herald* in 1842 depicts him in a scholarly pose, a man with a broad head and high brow, his hand on an open Bible—an appropriate image for the Baptist lay preacher born in Pittsfield, Massachusetts, who predicted the end of the world would occur in 1843. Miller based his calculations on the biblical books of Daniel and Revelation. His startling pronouncement, first made public in 1831, created a major stir in the 1830s and 1840s. This kind of prediction gets attention in every age.

Miller was the founder of a distinctive apocalyptic tradition in American religion. *Apocalyptic* is a term used to identify religious movements that focus on the expectation of an imminent end to the present world. Individuals preoccupied with the apocalypse often examine ancient prophecies or contemporary events as clues or signs leading to the end. A sense of urgency commonly drives those who are part of these movements. Apocalyptic traditions typically draw heavily on biblical texts, especially the books of Ezekiel, Daniel, and Revelation, for their imagery and symbolism.

William Miller had not always been a serious student of the Bible. In fact, from 1804 to 1816 his reading of contemporary authors convinced him that the Bible was no different from other books written by human authors. During those years he became a Deist, someone who accepted the reality of God but rejected much of the institutional religion of Miller's day. He emphasized the importance of moral activity rather than conventional devotional practices. Miller fought against England in the War of 1812 and served in the army from 1813 until 1815. His wartime experiences, including participation in the battle of Plattsburgh Bay, affected him deeply. The surprising victory at Plattsburgh against the overwhelming military advantage of the British convinced him that God was on the side of the Americans, and that reflection led to a period of intense spiritual struggle.

In 1816 Miller found freedom from his inner anguish: He turned his back on the Deists and returned to the religious views of his youth. Later, in a recollection published in 1842, he wrote, "While I was a Deist, I believed in a God, but I could not, as I thought, believe that the Bible was the word of God." Following his change of heart, the Bible became his "chief study," and he "searched it with great delight," especially its prophetic sections. From those texts Miller concluded that "the end of all things was clearly and emphatically predicted, both as to time and manner." The biblical passages that fascinated him told of the physical return of Christ in the clouds of heaven, the destruction of the earth by fire, and the salvation of the righteous, who would subsequently reign with Christ.

This end-time scenario lay hidden in the Bible's apocalyptic texts, writings that profess to reveal the future.

Miller, a farmer by trade, was consumed with the study of apocalyptic passages. He thought that the twenty-three hundred days mentioned in Daniel 8:14 referred to the purification of the earth by fire. Miller believed that in the Bible's apocalyptic passages "days" could be read as "years"; he dated the beginning of the 2,300 years to 457 B.C.E., when the Persian king Arta-xerxes commanded that Jerusalem be rebuilt after its earlier destruction by the Babylonians. Arithmetic did the rest: 457 subtracted from 2,300 equaled the year C.E. 1843.

By 1823 Miller had worked out the details of his apocalyptic calculations, correlating biblical prophecies with historical and contemporary events. But he had little success in converting others to his views. Strangely enough, he was timid and reluctant to talk about these matters. That situation continued until August 1831, when he was invited to preach in Dresden, Vermont. On this particular occasion his proclamation that Christ was coming soon struck a responsive chord and affected many in the audience. Shortly after that, Miller began receiving more invitations to lecture than he was able to accept.

Miller preached and lectured constantly, and in many locations local revivals—periods of spiritual intensity and heightened religious concern—followed. In the spring of 1832 he published a series of articles in the *Vermont Telegraph* detailing his views on the Second Coming, a traditional apocalyptic idea that Christ was to return physically to the earth. A pamphlet followed in 1834 and then a book entitled *Evidence from Scripture and History of the Second Coming of Christ, about the Year 1843: Exhibited in a Course of Lectures* (1836).

During these years Miller confined his travels to rural New England, northern New York, and Canada. That was to change, however, after he met Joshua V. Himes at a conference in Exeter, New Hampshire. Himes, the minister at the Chardon Street Chapel in Boston, invited Miller to lecture at his church, which he did twice a day to large audiences. Himes was active in a variety of reform movements, including the causes of antislavery, temperance, peace, and women's rights. Within a short time he became the leading advocate of *Millerism*, the term a rising number of opponents used to ridicule William Miller's Adventist message, that is, his proclamation of the Second Coming, or advent, of Christ.

Himes quickly emerged as the principal organizer and promoter of the Adventist movement. He began to publish a newspaper, *Signs of the Times*, in the spring of 1840, followed shortly by another publication, *The Second Advent*. He organized a conference at his church in Boston in October focusing on the "gospel of the kingdom at hand." Himes raised money to finance the distribution of literature—books, pamphlets, and tracts throughout the nation, and was involved in the compilation and publication of an Adventist hymnbook. He scheduled a series of general conferences at locations throughout the East. All of these activities brought heightened attention to the Adventist cause.

By the spring of 1842 pressures mounted on Miller to fix a specific date for the Second Coming. After some reluctance he agreed and declared that the return of Christ, an event that also would signal the end of the present world, would occur between March 21, 1843, and March 21, 1844. Those dates provided new incentive for believers to spread the Adventist gospel. Himes and his associates distributed thousands of publications, organized Adventist libraries, created prophetic charts, edited yet another newspaper, the *Midnight Cry*, planned a series of outdoor revival meetings known as camp meetings, constructed a great tent that seated thousands for those meetings, and dispatched scores of traveling ministers to warn of the impending physical return of Christ. Miller lectured tirelessly on behalf of the cause, proclaiming the coming of the Lord.

The larger the Adventist movement became, the harsher the response of its critics. Newspapers published by religious denominations denounced the Millerites, charging Miller, Himes, and other leaders with insincerity and financial exploitation of their followers. Skeptics made fun of the Adventist message and ridiculed those who accepted it. Critics accused Millerism of contributing to a host of social ills, including destruction of families, poverty, and mental illness. None of this opposition dissuaded those who watched and waited eagerly.

The opening months of 1843 saw Adventist fervor reach new heights. Secular newspapers carried advertisements for literature published by proponents of the cause urging readers to "prepare to meet their God" as well as articles by opponents designed to refute the apocalyptic calculations of Miller's followers. People of all persuasions were talking about the end of the world. Thousands gathered at camp meetings. Adventists built *tabernacles*—buildings designed especially for their meetings—in Boston and at other sites to accommodate the crowds. They also watched for unusual "signs of the times" that might indicate the coming of Christ. For example, the unexpected appearance of a comet on February 28 quickened the pulse of those waiting and convinced still more of the truth of the Adventist message. Some believers abandoned their regular occupations and spent their days trying to convince others of the need to prepare. As the months of 1843 passed, the intensity of activity increased. Adventists reported conversions to the cause from every corner of the nation. Miller mania was rampant throughout the United States.

And then the date came and passed, and disappointment set in among believers. Even Miller confessed disappointment at his miscalculation and apologized publicly, but he did not give up his faith that Christ would come soon. Critics heaped scorn on the Adventists, issuing false reports of people driven mad by fear and of others left standing on hilltops dressed in white robes. Scoffers mocked the faith of those who had hoped to meet the returning Christ.

But often hope that disappoints is not abandoned completely, and that was the case with the Adventists. During the summer of 1844 some who had waited looked for new developments. One preacher, Samuel S. Snow, using an elaborate set of calculations involving the Jewish, or lunar, calendar instead of the Gregorian calendar, announced a new date for the end of the world—October 22, 1844. Miller and Himes were slow to join him, but when they saw the revived wave of excitement sweeping through the ranks, they could not resist. Adventists around the country again prepared for the end, some working feverishly to spread the word, others abandoning normal activities to get their affairs in order. The weeks in October saw continuous religious meetings in some locations.

On October 22 Adventists everywhere gathered for prayer and song to await the fulfillment of the prophecy. One favorite chorus, as reported in the *New York Morning Express*, included the refrain "We're going! We're going! We're on our journey home!" But at the end of the day, rather than going to their heavenly home, the twice disappointed simply trudged back to their earthly homes, their hope of meeting Christ again thwarted. The Adventist cause suffered a crushing blow with this Great Disappointment, leaving its leader again keenly disappointed, and most of his followers disillusioned with prophecy. The Millerites were targets of a new round of ridicule, scorn, and physical harassment. Miller, dejected and dismayed, died in 1849, though he never abandoned his belief that Christ's return was imminent. Most of his followers forsook the cause; only a few clung to the Adventist gospel.

Why would anyone continue to subscribe to this failed prophecy? One of those who did not abandon her conviction concerning the Second Coming was Ellen Harmon. She was a native of Maine whose family accepted Adventist teaching and lived through the Great Disappointment. In 1844, the teenaged Harmon experienced a vision in which she traveled toward the heavenly city along with other Adventists. The journey was difficult, and many grew weary and gave up. After some time in paradise, she returned to earth. In her vision she also observed the dead rising from their graves and ascending to heaven.

Soon Ellen was relating her visions to others. These were the circumstances under which she met James White, a former Adventist preacher. In 1846 they married and began traveling together, meeting with former followers of William Miller, trying to reassure them of eventual triumph. At this time the Whites adopted Sabbatarian views, the belief that the proper day to worship is Saturday rather than Sunday.

But biblical prophecy remained the heart of the Whites' religious concerns as they and other former Adventists struggled to salvage the apocalyptic message of Christ's return. A colleague, Hiram Edson of Port Gibson, New York, led them to believe that the date October 22, 1844, had been correct; the mistake involved the location of Christ's activity, which was not on earth, but rather in heaven. This reinterpretation provided a way to rationalize and overcome the disappointment that resulted from anticipating a physical return of Christ. For a time during the following years they also believed that only those who had accepted Adventism before October 22, 1844, could have access to salvation. The door was shut for all others. The Whites held this belief for several years until they came to recognize that many outside their circle wanted to accept the Adventist gospel.

The Whites were a successful team: Ellen the visionary and prophetess, James the organizer and publisher. Ellen experienced visions relating to doctrine and behavior, and James published periodicals to spread the Sabbatarian Adventist message, including the *Second Advent Review and Sabbath Herald*. Among their leading doctrines were belief in the return of Christ, acceptance of the seventh-day Sabbath, and acknowledgment of the authority of the Bible. By the early 1860s they organized the movement as a new denomination with its center in Battle Creek, Michigan, under the name of the Seventh-day Adventist Church.

Ellen White's fervent hope for the return of Christ did not lead to a life of inactivity. On the contrary, a full agenda of reform causes filled her days of watching and waiting. Ellen's recurrent illnesses—a severe childhood injury and a variety of maladies, including headaches, fainting spells, heart problems, and nervousness—kept her preoccupied with matters of sickness and health. In the early 1850s she and her followers turned to prayer for assistance rather than to doctors and medications.

By the end of the decade, however, Ellen modified her attitude, in part because of negative publicity resulting from the death of an Adventist who had received no medical attention. In 1860 she announced her changed views and allowed for the treatment of illness by the use of both prayer and physicians. On June 6, 1863, Ellen had a vision relating to health care, urging moderation in the consumption of food and drink. She opposed the use of drugs commonly prescribed by physicians of the day, including opium, mercury, and strychnine, as well as dependence upon stimulants such as coffee and tea, and she cautioned about eating meat. She called for simple foods and a vegetarian diet, reflecting ideas popular at the time. For example, one prominent health reformer, Sylvester Graham, had argued for the virtues of whole wheat flour, a type of flour we still associate with the graham cracker.

Ellen White's prescription for healthfulness featured natural remedies, including the use of "God's great medicine, water, pure soft water, for diseases, for health, for cleanliness, and for luxury." She became a strong advocate of the water cure—hydropathy, as it was called—a popular form of alternative health practice in the nineteenth century. Hydropathy prescribed the application of water in every possible way—drinking, bathing, soaking, and even hosing. The Whites became strong proponents of hygienic living—another term for the approach to health care that included hydropathic therapeutics—which they trumpeted in Adventist publications.

They visited the famed water-cure retreat, Our Home on the Hillside, in Dansville, New York. These experiences became the model the Whites subsequently adopted when in 1866 they opened their own facility, the Western Health Reform Institute in Battle Creek, Michigan, the first of many institutions combining Adventist religious beliefs and health reforms.

Ellen White's interests in healthful living took another direction, too, namely, the support of dress reform. Feminists in the 1850s launched a campaign to free women from the tortures of tight corsets, hoopskirts, and heavy petticoats. The pioneers of dress reform adopted the bloomer, a short skirt over full loose trousers gathered at the ankles, as an answer to the problem and a signal of support for women's rights. Ellen White's reaction to traditional dress was negative, but not for the same reasons as those of the bloomerites. She had always favored modesty in dress for religious reasons, but she feared that wearing the "American costume," a short dress and trousers combination, would result in a masculine appearance and thus discredit the Adventists on yet more grounds.

On this matter, too, however, Ellen slowly changed her mind. In 1867 an angel in a vision showed her a dress length that was "modest, healthful, and cleared the filth of the street and sidewalk" by a few inches. She adapted the bloomer to fit her own sense of the proper, dropping the skirt to eight inches or so from the floor, but this Adventist version of dress reform never gained widespread acceptance. The costume embarrassed women, and men disliked the shorter skirt because of its association with the cause of women's rights. Within the church it proved an issue of unending controversy, with the result that on January 3, 1875, Ellen received a vision instructing her to end the effort to reform women's dress.

One other activity in which Adventists invested heavily was Christian education. Ellen White believed that religious instruction ought to be accompanied by practical education. After considerable discussion within the denomination, in 1874 the church opened Battle Creek College, the first of many educational institutions sponsored by the denomination.

Seven years later James White died unexpectedly, sending Ellen into a deep depression. After she emerged from a period of mourning, she spent much of the next two decades traveling in Europe, Australia, and New Zealand, founding Seventh-day Adventist institutions and working on behalf of the causes she valued so highly. She also continued to publish testimonies containing the divine messages she received. Upon her return to America in 1900, she settled in California, where she remained active for fifteen more years in the leadership of the church, publishing and supporting its work in the fields of health, education, and evangelism. What began with the visions of a seventeen-year-old in the aftermath of the Great Disappointment, by 1900 had become a worldwide community of more than sixty-seven thousand members. By the end of the twentieth century the total membership approached five million.

Not all nineteenth-century prophetic movements accommodated so easily to the world around them. The closing decades of the century witnessed the birth of another American apocalyptic sect, a group founded by Charles Taze Russell. Born in Pittsburgh, Russell was of Presbyterian background. He joined his father as a business partner in a clothing store, and they were very successful. But the same years saw him grow uncertain about his beliefs, abandoning the Presbyterians and exploring other options.

In 1869 Russell encountered an Adventist preacher in Allegheny, Pennsylvania. That experience piqued his interest, and with some friends he began serious study of the Bible. He also read a newspaper entitled *Bible Examiner*, published by George Storrs, a former follower of William Miller. Storrs was a direct line of influence connecting early Adventism and the apocalyptic movement Russell was to found, a movement he did not name initially. Eventually this organization would become the Jehovah's Witnesses. In the 1870s Russell published a pamphlet, *The Object and Manner of Our Lord's Return*, which argued for the notion of Christ returning invisibly to earth before the battle identified in the Bible as Armageddon, the final conflict of good and evil. He took that idea from Storrs. Eventually they distributed fifty-thousand copies of the publication.

Russell's subsequent association with another independent Adventist preacher, Nelson H. Barbour, led him further into the intricacies of prophecy. He accepted Barbour's calculations that Christ's invisible return had occurred in 1873 and that the following year marked the beginning of the "harvest," a traditional apocalyptic metaphor for the last years of the present world. Russell financed publication of a book by Barbour entitled *Three Worlds and the Harvest of This World* (1877), which used apocalyptic texts to determine the dates for Christ's visible return and the restoration of earth to a state of paradise. Barbour marked 1878 and 1914 as significant years—1878 was when the righteous would be "raptured," or rescued miraculously, from tribulation on earth, and 1914 was to be the conclusion of the harvest. The failure of the rapture to occur broke this alliance, and Russell launched a new periodical,

Zion's Watch Tower and Herald of Christ's Presence, in 1879. From this point on he developed increasingly independent views.

Russell never escaped the inclination to set dates. For example, he quickly reset the date of the rapture for 1881, but then issued a reinterpretation of his prediction, suggesting that he meant it might happen anytime after that year. Nonetheless, he displayed a remarkable confidence in his apocalyptic calculations, and he persuaded many others, including his new wife, Maria Frances Ackley. Pastor Russell, as he became known, was tireless in his efforts. He traveled widely, lecturing and organizing study groups. He wrote and published a stream of materials, estimated by the end of his life to have totaled fifty-thousand printed pages. The distribution of his tracts and books was enormous. At first he had no intention of establishing a new sect or denomination. But his religious ideas provoked opposition from mainstream churches, forcing him toward a separate organization, known first simply as Bible Students and sometimes as Russellites. By 1884 the group's official name was Zion's Watch Tower Tract Society.

Even before that date Russell and his followers repudiated a number of traditional Christian doctrines. They rejected the time-honored Christian view of God, suggesting that Jesus was not God but rather a created being who died as a ransom paid to the devil. Similarly, they did not accept the belief in hell, declaring rather that the unrighteous die and are annihilated instead of suffering eternally in hell. Russell, who was regarded as an end-time messenger, proclaimed Christ's Second Coming, a severe negative judgment on the nations of the world, and the inevitable defeat of Satan's forces at Armageddon in 1914.

Russell also proved a master of the printed page, publishing six volumes in the Millennial Dawn series between 1886 and 1904. Bible Students distributed nearly five million copies from the series in addition to a huge number of tracts and periodicals. They also took advantage of new technologies, including phonograph records, to spread the apocalyptic message. Russell himself traveled throughout North America and Europe on behalf of the cause, earning the respect and affection of his followers.

But he also experienced hostility and opposition, some from within the movement and more from without. Internal hostility came from an unexpected source, his wife, Maria, who in the late 1890s quarreled with Russell and subsequently attacked his authority and character. She accused him of being the "evil servant" of Matthew 24:48—who is described as one who says in his heart, "My lord delayeth his coming"—and of being a tyrant. The two disagreed on the proper role of women in marriage. Their conflict ultimately became a public scandal and ended in divorce in 1903. External opposition came largely from clergy whom Russell had denounced as false shepherds. They accused him of adultery, or engaging in sexual relations with someone other than his wife; fraud; and perjury, or lying under oath. The secular press joined the attacks. Russell was in court repeatedly during his later years, involved in legal suits that he launched against detractors and defending himself against charges brought against him for failure to pay support to Maria after their divorce.

As 1914, the date predicted by Russell for the destruction of the world and the beginning of Christ's millennial reign, approached, excitement mounted among his followers. But this time he had created a fail-safe device for dealing with

Fig. 1: In this 1693 woodcut, Cotton Mather stands in the center of a magic circle to protect himself from the devil. Mather, considered an expert on magic and witchcraft because of his publications, is trying to instruct the devil about the truth—a hopeless task, one would assume.

Fig. 2: The Friends Meetinghouse in Golansville, Virginia, was spare and simple. Following Quaker patterns established in colonial times, men and women sat in silence and waited for the Spirit to give them a message to share with their fellow Friends.

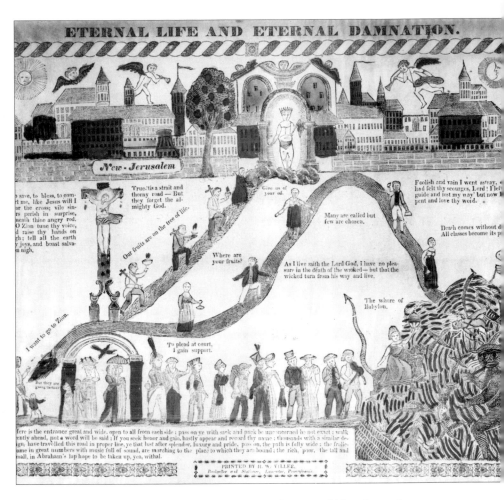

Fig. 3: George Rapp's vision of alternative paths to eternal life and eternal damnation required members of the Harmony Society to follow the "strait and thorny" road to the New Jerusalem.

Fig. 4: Anti-Millerite cartoons ridiculed Adventist believers and their ideas. A Millerite awaiting the earth's destruction hides, ironically, in a safe stockpiled with cheese, crackers, and other foodstuffs, and thumbs his nose at nonbelievers.

Fig. 5: Shaker sisters toiled in the herb industry, producing medicinal extracts for sale in the outside world. Their labor was a critical contribution to the society's economic success.

Fig. 6: Seventh-day Adventists, both men and women, in conventional street clothing, take part in physical exercises at Battle Creek, Michigan, the headquarters of the movement. Health and physical fitness were preoccupations of this religious movement.

Fig. 7: This early prophetic chart, designed by an Adventist minister, depicts the chronology of the apocalyptic visions in the biblical books of Daniel and Revelation. Strange animals, ferocious beasts, mounted warriors, and trumpeting angels mark the passage of time on the chart.

July 15, 1983

The Watchtower
Announcing Jehovah's Kingdom

FEAR
A Sign of the End?

Fig. 8: Jehovah's Witnesses distribute millions of copies of each issue of The Watchtower, *the primary, biweekly publication of the organization. The cover of the July 15, 1983, issue juxtaposes the atomic mushroom cloud with explicit hints of an apocalyptic end of the world.*

Fig. 9: Members of the Peace Mission Movement, both black and white, ate at Father Divine's table, whether they could pay for the food or not. Hymns of praise rose from these worshipers who celebrated Divine's virtues.

Fig. 10: *Mary Baker Eddy, the founder of Christian Science, sat for this portrait around 1882, three years after she had founded the Church of Christ, Scientist. A year later she would launch* The Christian Science Journal, *the church's first periodical.*

Fig. 11: *On June 13, 1998, couples filled New York City's Madison Square Garden to receive the blessing of the Reverend Sun Myung Moon. Controversy surrounding these ceremonies stems from the fact that marriages are arranged by the Unification Church.*

Fig. 12: These children were some of the youngest Raja Yoga students at Point Loma, California. Katherine Tingley's approach to education aimed to transform the whole person—body, mind, spirit, and emotions.

Fig. 13: The scene in Guyana was almost beyond belief—the bodies of more than nine hundred members of the Peoples Temple, followers of Jim Jones, lying in the jungle clearing. The mass murder/suicide in Jonestown fueled an outburst of anticult sentiments and recriminations.

prophetic failure. The possibility of error or miscalculation, he affirmed, did not mean the events would not happen soon. The outbreak of the First World War in 1914 proved convenient, and he quickly interpreted it as confirming his predictions. But the war brought new problems for members of the group who were not willing to take part in the military effort. Many spent time in prison for their refusal to participate. Russell, whose most famous saying was "Millions now living will never die," died in October 1916 while traveling on behalf of the movement.

The end of the war brought peace to the nations in Europe rather than Armageddon. Russell's movement, numbering nearly fifteen thousand members worldwide, went through a period of internal turmoil as various individuals vied for leadership. Eventually Joseph Franklin Rutherford, a lawyer and disciple of Russell, assumed leadership of the movement and carried the Watch Tower Bible and Tract Society into the postwar period. In 1931 he renamed it the Jehovah's Witnesses.

The religious views of the Witnesses are still in sharp tension with those of most Americans. Members continue to live in expectation of an imminent end to the world. The message that they proclaim in publications and in person contains a harsh critique of other churches, the governments of the world, and many principal social organizations, including corporations and educational institutions. The Witnesses live in anticipation of a final catastrophic battle between the forces of good and evil, which will be followed by the transformation of earth into a paradiselike setting for the righteous and faithful. Contemporary Witnesses refuse to participate in military service; they also reject blood transfusions because they regard the latter as a violation of Old Testament regulations against imbibing blood. They continue to enjoy success in the United States and throughout the world, though they often are the objects of hatred, violence, and persecution. In 1999 their membership worldwide approached eight million.

The United States proved very hospitable to the rise of apocalyptic sects in the nineteenth century. Even when prophecies failed, religious outsiders did not give up hope, watching and waiting for the end. Many continue to do so.

Apocalyptic movements are often associated with dire predictions and warnings concerning the future. Pessimism is the dominant mood in such prophecies, but there is another side to such matters for the faithful. In the preface to one of the volumes in the Millennial Dawn series, Charles Taze Russell warns his readers of the approaching day of Jehovah, but counsels those of the "household of faith" not to be discouraged by the times of crisis.

We have already shown that the time is at hand, and that the events of the day of Jehovah are even now crowding close upon us. A few years more must of necessity ripen the elements now working in the direction of the predicted trouble; and, according to the sure word of prophecy, the present generation will witness the terrible crisis and pass through the decisive conflict.

It is not our purpose, in calling attention to this subject, to arouse a mere sensation, or to seek to gratify idle curiosity. Nor can we hope to produce that penitence in the hearts of men which would work a change in the present social, political and religious order of society, and thus avert the impending calamity. The approaching trouble is inevitable: the powerful causes are all at work, and no human power is able to arrest their operation and progress toward the certain end: the effects must follow as the Lord foresaw and foretold. No hand but the hand of God could stay the progress of the present current of events; and his hand will not do so until the bitter experiences of this conflict shall have sealed their instruction upon the hearts of men.

The main object of this volume is not, therefore, to enlighten the world, which can appreciate only the logic of events and will have no other; but to forewarn, forearm, comfort, encourage and strengthen "the household of faith," so that they may not be dismayed, but may be in full harmony and sympathy with even the severest measures of divine discipline in the chastening of the world, seeing by faith the glorious outcome in the precious fruits of right-eousness and enduring peace.

CHAPTER FIVE

Healers and Occultists: Women of Spiritual Means

I n the United States of the nineteenth century women rarely occupied formal positions of religious leadership. In the mainstream churches—Protestant and Catholic—the ranks of the clergy were almost exclusively a male domain. The few exceptions to this pattern provoked heated controversy.

Alternative religions, by contrast, often provided opportunities for females to exercise religious authority. Quaker women, for example, spoke within the meetings, gained a reputation for their spirituality, and served as "traveling Friends." Ann Lee was the founder of the Shakers, and women exercised considerable leadership within that community. Ellen White was the dominant force in the development of the Seventh-day Adventist Church for more than half a century. But controversy surrounded these women.

Other outsider groups also had women in major leadership roles. Alternative movements often provided women possessing special knowledge and understanding, or insight and wisdom, opportunities to exert authority and influence. In these communities religion commonly empowered women.

Imagine the excitement that filled the small town of Hydesville, New York, in early 1848, when two young sisters, Margaret and Kate Fox, began to hear mysterious rappings in their house. Before long the girls linked the sounds to spirit forces operating in their midst. Fifteen and twelve years old, the two worked out a system of communication with the spirits by snapping their fingers and asking questions. The answers came in more knocks. Terror and curiosity alternated among family members and neighbors. The girls were separated for a time and sent to live with relatives, but the sounds followed them. Then came a more elaborate communication system that involved rapping out the alphabet.

Word of these strange happenings spread, and many came to see the Fox sisters and hear the rappings. Newspaper accounts circulated the story across the nation. The crowds that came included both those who wanted to believe in the spirits and those who were skeptical. Efforts to investigate this mystery fueled even more public interest. Before the end of 1849 the Fox sisters were filling a large hall in Rochester with an audience that paid admission to witness demonstrations. Further inquiries by journalists and clergy did nothing to dampen the excitement.

In June 1850 the Fox family went to New York City and held a series of public séances. Séances are gatherings convened for the purpose of communicating with the spirits, presided over by a medium, or someone knowledgeable about the spirit world and capable of mediating between it and this world. People paid to participate in these séances, which seemed to reinforce the believers in their belief and the skeptics in their skepticism. One believer, Horace Greeley, editor of the *New York Weekly Tribune*, defended the Fox sisters in his newspaper. Other journalists leveled charges of fraud against them.

One unexpected and unplanned result of these rappings was the growth of an expanding number of individuals and groups intent on communicating with the spirit world. Circles formed among those who wanted to believe in the possibility and the reality of spirit communication. Doubters became all the more determined to expose the deceit they assumed lay behind the knocks and the claims of the mediums.

One set of investigators from a medical school in Buffalo, New York, after visiting with the Fox sisters, concluded that the girls produced the raps by muscular snapping of their joints. Even some believers found the doctors' explanation plausible. Yet that judgment did little to dissuade those who saw the efforts to communicate with spirits as confirmation of the hope of life after death, a hope they held dear. Not even the disclosure in 1851 by a relative of the Fox girls that the sisters had, indeed, made the noises by voluntarily snapping their toe joints could discourage the believers.

The spiritualist movement (also known as Spiritualism) began with these unusual events in Hydesville. The movement expanded rapidly for reasons that had little to do with Margaret and Kate Fox. In fact, the story of the Fox sisters in the years following was a narrative filled with complex and tragic personal problems.

Tens of thousands of Americans took part in séances, formed spiritualist circles, attended public meetings where mediums communicated with spirits or lectured while in a trance, and subscribed to spiritualist periodicals. Through these actions they were affirming their belief in the afterlife, their conviction that personal identity did not end with death, and their hope that friendships and family relationships formed in this world would continue into another reality. In the spiritualist movement they found reassurance concerning the Christian doctrines of the resurrection, immortality of the soul, and the existence of eternal rewards and punishments in heaven and hell. Most who took part regarded Spiritualism and Christianity as compatible systems of belief.

Mediums provided believers with apparent proof of personal existence after death. The proof appeared almost scientific. Spirits "caused" chairs and tables to move, lights to dim, and buildings to creak. They answered specific questions with knowledge not readily available. The physical signs and messages received during séances or spirit meetings seemed to prove victory over death and to give reason for ultimate optimism. The presence of spirits, therefore, was generally more comforting than frightening.

Interest in Spiritualism was never restricted to a particular level of society. On more than one occasion Mary Todd Lincoln, wife of Abraham Lincoln, brought mediums into the White House to assist in communicating with her dead children. For example, following the death of her son Willie, Mrs. Lincoln consulted with a spiritualist who conveyed messages from him. President Lincoln apparently was not particularly interested in these séances. In later life Mary Todd Lincoln's mental instability resulted in commitment to an insane asylum, where she attempted suicide. The grounds for her commitment included judgments concerning her behavior that listed claims of unusual communications.

Spiritualists in the nineteenth century did not establish conventional churches with clergy as their leaders. The organizational side of the movement was more fluid. Believers gathered regularly in small circles under the guidance of a local medium. Members of these circles usually retained their membership in established churches. Other spiritualists took part in séances conducted by professional mediums who charged for their services. Many others attended mass meetings led by celebrated mediums.

More women than men presided as mediums at spiritualist gatherings of all kinds. This movement provided women a direct avenue to public religious leadership. At the middle of the century it was still highly controversial for women to speak in public to an audience composed of both men and women. Conventional conservative views limited women's activities to the home and church, although they were not allowed to become ministers. But within a short period of time female mediums were performing and lecturing in front of large paying audiences. Empowered by special gifts and spiritual sensitivities, these women carried out tasks normally reserved for male clergy, and they enjoyed great success.

The séances and public spiritualist meetings were highly entertaining. Attractive young women serving as mediums and dressed in fashionable clothes, held the attention of spectators for hours as they spoke in a trance, described visions of angels, or delivered messages from dead relatives. Audiences came expecting to see and hear the unusual, and they were rarely disappointed. Mediums and trance speakers became celebrities, and they attracted a following. One observer, writing in 1859, described Cora Hatch, a prominent medium, as "a delicate-featured blond, of seventeen or eighteen, [with] flaxen ringlets falling over her shoulders." Hatch commonly conducted her meetings in a trance, while "gazing upward, with her eyes intently fixed."

This entertainment dimension led to crass imitations of spiritualist meetings. People with little or no interest in things spiritual held meetings at which they copied the actions of mediums. These occasions were motivated by amusement and commercial gain. Imitators fueled further charges by opponents of the movement that the spiritualists, too, were fraudulent.

Female mediums were at the center of attention and controversy. They were widely admired by those who turned to them for counsel and advice. Their ability to communicate with the spirit world was a special religious credential. At the same time these women were often the object of sustained criticism and public attack because they defied the social and religious conventions of the day. They refused to be governed by the notions of proper behavior for the sexes.

Some mediums added to their problems by advocating radical social ideas. For instance, some criticized marriage as a social institution and proposed the alternative practice of free love, a term that in the nineteenth century covered a variety of ideas and practices, including the notion that sexual relations did not have to be confined to marriage. Other female spiritualists argued for the principle of radical self-determination for women. Women's rights were therefore a favorite cause for many mediums. One prominent spiritualist, Julia Branch, voiced her criticism of established practices by suggesting that in marriage the woman lost "control of her name, her person, her property, her labor, her affections, her children, and her freedom." For that reason Branch and others found the spiritualist movement both empowering and consistent with the most radical efforts on behalf of women's rights in the mid-nineteenth century.

Another new religious movement that empowered women in important ways arose from the personal circumstances of its founder, Mary Baker Eddy. Known today as Christian Science, this movement first took institutional form in 1879 in Lynn, Massachusetts, where Eddy and twenty-seven followers organized the first Church of Christ, Scientist. But the ideas at the heart of this new sect were the product of the more than fifty years of the founder's life preceding that moment.

Eddy was born Mary Baker into a middle-class family in Bow, New Hampshire. During her childhood and adolescence, she experienced prolonged periods of debilitating physical and psychological illness that kept her from school and other activities. In response, she concentrated her attention on reading and writing. At the age of twenty-two, she married George Glover, a building contractor and friend of the family. They moved to South Carolina, where he died within a year. Mary Baker Glover gave birth to a son after she returned to New England, but she proved unable to care for him, and he was given to foster parents. In 1853 she married Daniel Patterson, an itinerant dentist who turned out to be unreliable and probably unfaithful. During this marriage Mary Baker Patterson often found herself alone and ill while Patterson was pursuing his profession. Her suffering—both physical and mental—continued for years until 1873, when she obtained a divorce.

Throughout the years of constant difficulty, Mary Baker Patterson nurtured her interest in writing and searched for some therapy that would heal her. She experimented with a variety of spiritual and therapeutic movements: homeopathy, a medical system based on small doses of drugs that produced the symptoms of the illness; the water cure, a therapy that applied water in every possible way in pursuit of health; mesmerism, a treatment that employed hypnotism and suggestion; and Spiritualism. In 1862 her search led her to Phineas Parkhurst Quimby, who healed patients by inspiring them with a positive mental attitude. She derived almost immediate benefit from studying with him and from his "science of health" that emphasized mind cure, and as a result she began to experience new energy and well-being.

But according to her autobiography written many years later, entitled *Retrospection and Introspection*, Mary Baker Patterson came to her new insights into health and spiritual wholeness by reading the Bible. She recalled a serious fall on the ice in 1866 from which doctors gave her little chance of recovery. While in that perilous state she read the New Testament accounts of Jesus' miracles, recognized the spiritual nature of his healings, and recovered immediately. That great discovery, as she termed it, became the center of her life. She set out to clarify and teach the healing method she had discovered and experienced.

The next several years were still very difficult, for Mary Baker Patterson had no financial security. She moved frequently from place to place, often depending on the generosity of friends. Yet these years saw her continue to write and rewrite her ideas, struggling to formulate her insights into healing.

Even in these desperate circumstances she began to attract disciples. With their help, in 1875 she published the first edition of *Science and Health*, her attempt to state clearly and definitively her ideas concerning God, the world, and the science of healing. In 1877 she married Asa Eddy, a sewing machine salesman and one of her first converts. He died five years later of heart disease.

Science and Health was published in many editions during Eddy's lifetime as she struggled to refine and edit her "textbook"—a term she and her followers used to describe the centrality of this publication in their lives. It represented a reformulation of Christian thought and a radical departure from conventional religious ideas.

Mary Baker Eddy based Christian Science on her reinterpretation of the Bible. She rejected the assumptions informing much of nineteenth-century Protestantism, the tradition she had known as a child. She was, in particular, offended by the notion that God might be responsible for allowing suffering or sin in the world. On the contrary, Eddy and her followers affirmed the essential and absolute goodness of God. She declared God is All-in-all, and nothing exists apart from God. God is also Mind, not material being. And God is Life, Truth, and Love. Therefore, if God is Mind (the opposite of matter), and good (the opposite of evil), and all-embracing, then it follows logically and theologically that everything that exists is good and is part of the Divine Mind. Truth is the recognition of that fact and of its essential corollary, namely, that matter and evil cannot exist but rather are illusions. That does not mean illusions are not powerful. They are so long as they control. But when illusions, such as sin and sickness, are recognized as false, they lose their power. Then a healing process occurs and wholeness—both spiritual and physical—results.

Mainstream religious leaders at the end of the nineteenth century responded very negatively to Eddy and Christian Science. They charged her with delusions of grandeur and with being dictatorial and mercenary. She did charge fees to those who studied with her in order to become practitioners of Christian Science. Students of Quimby accused her of plagiarizing his writings. Some of her closest associates turned against her and revealed embarrassing inconsistencies between her public and private actions. At one point late in life her son George returned and attempted to gain control of her financial resources. Mark Twain directed some of his most acerbic writing against her and Christian Science, accusing both of gross commercialism. No doubt these attacks were part of the reason that in her last years she withdrew from public view and retreated into relative isolation, making known her judgments and decisions from afar.

Eddy was remarkably successful during the second half of her life. She went from poverty to riches, from suffering to success, from obscurity to fame. In 1881 she founded the Massachusetts Metaphysical College to teach her ideas and her method of healing to her followers. She managed to finance successfully two buildings for the Mother Church in Boston, one in 1894 and another in 1906. Her publications multiplied with the passage of years, because she wrote almost continuously. In 1908 she initiated the effort that led to the establishment of the *Christian Science Monitor*, a newspaper that might provide a public journalistic defense of the movement against its detractors.

Christian Scientists attempted to live in a manner consistent with the principles Eddy taught in *Science and Health*. They were to study the textbook and the Bible in order to understand the true nature of reality. That insight and understanding would then free them from the power of sin, sickness, and even death. As a practical matter, Christian Scientists employed spiritual healing rather than turning to doctors and conventional medicine. Prayer formed a part of this spiritual therapy, but understanding was even more central. Eddy wrote in *Science and Health*, "Therefore the divine Principle of Science, reversing the testimony of the physical senses, reveals man as harmoniously existent in Truth, which is the only basis of health; and thus Science denies all disease, heals the sick, overthrows false evidence, and refutes materialistic logic."

Eddy organized her movement in new and different ways. Each local branch of Christian Science was to follow the rules and procedures established in the *Church Manual*. There were no clergy or ministers. Each branch elected lay readers who served for limited terms of office. They did not preach but rather presided over the worship services, reading select excerpts from the Bible and *Science and Health*. Lay readers could be either men or women, and therefore this movement gave women opportunities for leadership closed to them in other churches. Women also could become Christian Science practitioners, individuals trained and credentialed by the church who work as professionals, assisting others in applying the teachings of the movement to their lives, especially in the area of healing. Christian Science established reading rooms where the publications of the church were readily available without cost to the public or where copies could also be purchased.

During her lifetime Eddy exercised tight control over the organization she founded, even after she retreated from the spotlight. Following her death she remained the Pastor Emeritus, and her plans for the organization remained in force through the influence of the *Church Manual.*

Christian Scientists accept Mary Baker Eddy's distinctive system of religious thought and the challenge of demonstrating its truthfulness in daily life. Healing is central to this movement, but the Christian Science concept of healing is broad and sweeping. Healing involves spiritual wholeness as well as physical well-being. Healing rests on understanding the true nature of God, of human beings, and of the surrounding world. That understanding is not obvious or commonsensical; it derives from an insight that comes through careful study and reflection on *Science and Health*, and in that respect it falls into the hidden or occult domain.

Christian Science attracted a significant number of converts during Eddy's lifetime. By 1906 some fifty-five thousand were members of the branches of the Church of Christ, Scientist. Some 72 percent of them were women. During the twentieth century Christian Science has repeatedly found itself under attack in the courts, most often in cases involving the medical treatment of children within the church. In recent decades the rising public concern regarding child neglect or abuse has triggered challenges to Christian Science parents who have been charged with various crimes. The church has consistently argued that its healing practices are effective. No clear pattern has emerged in the legal decisions. There have been some convictions, while other cases have been dismissed. All parties recognize that issues of religious freedom are involved.

The Mother Church does not issue contemporary membership statistics for Christian Science. Therefore no precise numbers exist at the present. Most informed observers, however, believe that this is a movement in numerical decline.

A third alternative religion involving the occult that proved empowering for women was Theosophy, a religious movement with links to Spiritualism that developed during the same period as Christian Science. Theosophy, in a generic sense, points to "knowledge of divine things" or "knowledge of God." In a particular sense, it refers to the Theosophical Society founded by Helena P. Blavatsky and Henry S. Olcott in New York City in 1875. The previous year Blavatsky and Olcott had met in Vermont at a site where spiritualists had reported the materialization of spirits or successful communication with spirits. The two became intimate friends. Blavatsky was a world traveler and an immigrant from Russia who arrived in America in 1874. Olcott was a lawyer and journalist who had served in the Union army during the Civil War. The organization they founded attracted a varied group of people interested in world religions, including Thomas Edison and Abner Doubleday, who is often credited as the inventor of baseball.

Blavatsky emerged as the chief spokesperson for the movement. In 1877 she published *Isis Unveiled*, a rambling account of the occult or hidden knowledge found in the world's religions and philosophies. She ranged widely over such diverse topics as magic, the brotherhood of legendary Masters who purportedly resided in the mountains of Tibet, as well as Hindu and Buddhist teachings. She presumed to open the secrets behind the religions of the world. She pointed to connections among them, thus reducing the claims to exclusiveness offered by some. Olcott spent his time and energy on the organizational side of the Theosophical Society.

Shortly after publication of *Isis Unveiled*, Blavatsky and Olcott traveled to India to gain further insight into Eastern religions and to establish the Theosophical Society in Asia. The Theosophical Twins, as they were called, spent the next six years in India, years that witnessed some successes organizationally, some charges of fraud directed against Blavatsky, and eventually a falling-out between the two founders. Blavatsky left Asia and traveled to Europe. She published *The Secret Doctrine* in London in 1888, three years before she died. This volume was a compendium of occultism, drawing on esoteric or supposedly secret materials from a wide range of the world's religions. Olcott stayed in Asia, where he exercised administrative control over the society.

Two female converts to Theosophy played important roles in the second generation of this movement. Annie Besant, an Englishwoman who entered the society in 1889, eventually succeeded Blavatsky and Olcott as the leader of the international organization. She was a highly talented person frustrated with the religious and social conventions of the day. An unsuccessful marriage, deep doubts about the doctrines of Christianity, resentment of the restrictive roles assigned to women—these factors fostered her interest in the Theosophical Society. Divorce, rejection of Christianity, and commitment to liberal causes followed. Besant was, for example, an early advocate of birth control. Her encounter with Blavatsky's *Secret Doctrine* led immediately to her conversion. She found in it what she had been searching for, a world view that combined faith and science. Subsequently she studied with Blavatsky and rose quickly in the ranks of the movement. Besant spoke as a representative of

Theosophy at the World's Parliament of Religions in Chicago in 1893. Under her leadership, following the death of Blavatsky, the society expanded to fifty-thousand members in forty countries by 1930, ten thousand of whom lived in the United States.

Katherine Tingley, an activist and reformer, emerged as the official leader of the society in the United States in 1898. She was the inspiration behind the Theosophical utopian community established at Point Loma in San Diego in 1897. This experiment was an undertaking that gained a wide reputation for its liberal efforts at child rearing and education, including the use of the Montessori system of instruction as well as the rich cultural programs it sponsored, including Greek dance. Point Loma underwent steady decline after her death and finally closed its doors in 1942.

The Theosophical Society was a genuine occult alternative because of its focus on hidden spiritual principles that were revealed through insightful teachers. As a movement, it represented a radical departure from the religious traditions that had dominated previously in the United States. It was one of the first channels through which Eastern religious ideas, both Hindu and Buddhist, entered this country and influenced non-Asian segments of the population. In that respect Theosophy anticipated developments that became much more significant in the religious history of the United States after World War II.

Spiritualists, Christian Scientists, and Theosophists—all three laid claim to special religious insight or hidden knowledge in different ways. Spiritualists claimed access to the world of spirits; Christian Scientists disclosed the secrets of spiritual healing; and Theosophists revealed the wisdom of the Masters. Each of these alternative religions enabled women to rise to positions of leadership and influence.

The ability to communicate with the spirits of the dead was the core belief of Spiritualism. Often that communication was unsettling, mysterious, and controversial. In no case was that truer than in the story of the Fox sisters as mediums. In 1848 the mother of Margaret and Kate Fox issued "A Report of the Mysterious Noises Heard in the House of Mr. John D. Fox in Wayne County," which suggests that spirits were communicating with her daughters through strange rappings.

We moved into this house on the 11th of December, 1847, and have resided here ever since. We formerly resided in the city of Rochester. We first heard this noise about a fortnight ago. It sounded like some one knocking in the east bedroom, on the floor; sometimes it sounded as if the chair moved on the floor; we could hardly tell where it was. This was in the evening, just after we had gone to bed. The whole family slept in that room together, and all heard the noise. There was four of our family, and sometimes five. The first night that we heard the rapping, we all got up and lit a candle; and searched all over the house. The noise continued while we were hunting, and was heard near the same place all the time. It was not very loud, yet it produced a jar of the bedsteads and chairs, that could be felt by placing our hands on the chair, or while we were in bed. It was a feeling of a tremulous motion, more than a sudden jar. It seemed as if we could feel it jar while we were standing on the floor. It continued this night until we went to sleep. I did not go to sleep until nearly 12 o'clock. The noise continued to be heard every night.

On Friday night, the 31st of March, it was heard as usual, and we then for the first time called in the neighbors. Up to this time we had never heard it in the day time, or at least did not notice it at all.

On Friday night we concluded to go to bed early, and not let it disturb us; if it came, we thought we would not mind it, but try and get a good night's rest. My husband was here on all these occasions, heard the noise and helped search. It was very early when we went to bed on this night; hardly dark. We went to bed so early, because we had been broken so much of our rest that I was almost sick.

My husband had not gone to bed when we first heard the noise on this evening. I had just laid down. It commenced as usual. I knew it from all other noises I had ever heard in the house. The girls, who slept in the other bed in the room, heard the noise, and tried to make a similar noise by snapping their fingers. The youngest girl is about 12 years old; she is the one who made her hand go. As fast as she made the noise with her hands or fingers, the sound was followed up in the room. It did not sound any different at that time, only it made the same number of noises that the girl did. When she stopped, the sound itself stopped for a short time.

The other girl, who is in her 15th year, then spoke in sport and said, "Now do this just as I do. Count one, two, three, four," &c., striking one hand in the other at the same time. The blows which she made were repeated as before. It appeared to answer her by repeating every blow that she made. She only did so once. She then began to be startled; and then I spoke and said to the noise, "Count ten," and it made ten strokes or noises. Then I asked the ages of my different children successively, and it gave a number of raps, corresponding to the ages of my children.

I then asked if it was a human being that was making the noise? and if it was, to manifest it by the same noise. There was no noise. I then asked if it was a spirit? and if it was, to manifest it by two sounds. I heard two sounds as soon as the words were spoken. . . .

CHAPTER SIX

Sectarians in the City

A ccording to the Pentecost experience of the first
Christians recorded in the biblical book of Acts, chapter 2, miraculous events occurred when the first disciples of
Christ were infused with God's Spirit. Tongues of fire appeared
on their heads, and a rushing wind filled the building. In
America Pentecostalism emerged on the national scene in a
depressed industrial area of Los Angeles in early 1906. The site
was 312 Azusa Street, where a dilapidated building that once
housed a Methodist mission stood. The revival that took place,
the Azusa Street revival, has been called the birth of modern
Pentecostalism. It was an outpouring of spiritual and ecstatic
activity that reminded participants and observers alike of the
original Pentecost. At Azusa, there were also signs and wonders. The gift of the Spirit was bestowed on participants who
spoke in unknown tongues. On both occasions those who took
part emerged from these experiences transformed and emboldened. This new movement in the United States named itself

the Apostolic Faith because of its similarity to the New Testament age of the apostles, or the first disciples of Christ.

The outpouring of spiritual gifts at Azusa stemmed directly from the earlier success of an independent Holiness preacher named Charles Fox Parham. The Holiness churches in the second half of the nineteenth century were based upon belief in an experience of *sanctification*, or receiving the power to live a holy or sanctified life, an experience that followed conversion to Christianity. Parham was among the first to speak about these ideas and call them the Apostolic Faith, thereby associating them with the early Christians. Parham, a Midwesterner, had drifted from the Methodists to the Holiness Church, and then to the Apostolic movement. In 1898 he established an institution in Topeka, Kansas, that solicited prayers for the sick. He also published a magazine entitled the *Apostolic Faith*. Two years later he founded Bethel Bible School, which emphasized portions of the Bible that suggested the notion that Christ's return to earth was about to happen. Bethel also focused on speaking in tongues as one of the gifts bestowed on Christians in the first century that was again available.

Parham's apostolic interests began to spread throughout the Midwest and elsewhere. In 1905 he established another Bible school in Houston that attracted like-minded individuals. It was there that William Joseph Seymour, the son of former slaves and an itinerant Holiness preacher who would become the principal figure in the Azusa Street revival, came under the influence of Parham and accepted the Apostolic Faith.

Early in 1906 Seymour left Houston and traveled to Los Angeles to serve an African-American Holiness mission. But he was unsuccessful in persuading its members to accept the

Apostolic Faith, and therefore he was without a congregation. In April 1906 Seymour himself spoke in tongues for the first time, and by that means he began to attract attention. Complaints followed when increasingly large groups of both blacks and whites attended a series of revival meetings he held. The songs, the shouting, and the crowds forced them to move to the Azusa Street address.

The Azusa Street revival lasted for three years. During this time thousands came to hear Seymour, to listen to the tongue-speaking, and to observe the signs and wonders taking place. Reports circulated about all manner of miraculous healings and ecstatic activity. On many days Seymour held three meetings. Azusa Street seemed the modern equivalent of the day of Pentecost.

"The meetings began about ten o'clock in the morning," wrote one observer in 1906 in the *Apostolic Faith*, "and can hardly stop before ten or twelve at night, and sometimes two or three in the morning, because so many are seeking, and some are slain under the power of God. People are seeking three times a day at the altar and row after row of seats have to be emptied and filled with seekers. We cannot tell how many people have been saved, and sanctified, and baptised with the Holy Ghost, and healed of all manner of sicknesses. Many are speaking in new tongues, and some are on their way to the foreign fields, with the gift of the language. We are going on to get more of the power of God."

The Azusa Street revival was interracial. Blacks and whites worshiped side by side, equally in the grasp of the Spirit and equally committed to tongue-speaking and the restoration of apostolic gifts. After some time the local newspaper began to feature events at the mission, which attracted more individuals to services. Before long other churches were imitating Azusa. In September 1907 Parham came to Los Angeles, but he was not happy with the unrestrained exuberance of the meetings or the interracial mix. When he tried to change things, he was rebuffed. By this point Azusa was generating a large amount of spiritual energy, and no one—not even Parham—could stifle that religious force.

The Azusa Street revival subsided after 1909, but the Pentecostal movement was only beginning. Seymour spent the remaining years of his life serving the congregation in Los Angeles, but the Apostolic Faith soon spread throughout the continent. That expansion is one of the remarkable stories of twentieth-century religious history. The apostolic revival did not produce only one Pentecostal sect but rather a host of groups. Among the sectarian organizations emerging from these beginnings are two denominations strong in the South: the Church of God (Cleveland, Tennessee), especially strong in North Carolina and Tennessee; and the Church of God in Christ, with its headquarters in Memphis, the largest Pentecostal denomination in the United States, composed primarily of African Americans.

Another important Pentecostal denomination is the Assemblies of God; it has the largest geographical spread of any U.S. Pentecostal community, including an aggressive missionary program abroad. The Pentecostal Assemblies of the World, an apostolic organization featuring opposition to the doctrine of the Trinity, teaches the oneness of God and requires baptism in the name of Jesus only. The United Pentecostal Church International, which teaches similar doctrine, split from the Pentecostal Assemblies of the World over racial issues, thereby becoming predominantly a white organization, leaving its parent group predominantly an African-American community. One other Pentecostal denomination, the International Church of the Foursquare Gospel, founded by the controversial preacher Aimee Semple McPherson and headquartered in Los Angeles, gained notoriety because of McPherson's sensational style of preaching. Sister Aimee was also involved in a highly publicized scandal involving an alleged kidnapping that turned out to be false. These and scores of smaller Pentecostal communities were the institutional results of the apostolic movement in the decades following the Azusa Street revival.

Pentecostals in all of these particular organizations shared certain common ideas and practices. The members of this movement believed that conversion or acceptance of Christianity must be followed by another experience, often called the baptism of the Spirit. This baptism—which is not water baptism—is made manifest or confirmed in the eyes of the community by reception of the apostolic gifts, most notably, speaking in tongues. Other spiritual gifts include healing, prophecy, and interpretation of tongues. These experiences are accessible to all individuals and do not require training, education, or special credentials. The worship services of this tradition express the same spirit-directed, ecstatic energy and spontaneity in music, testimony, and preaching.

The Pentecostal experience demonstrates that the arrival of the twentieth century did nothing to slow the growth of sects. NRMs continued to emerge with astonishing speed in the opening decades of the new century. The Constitution, after all, still guaranteed religious liberty. Waves of immigrants arriving in the United States from all parts of the world—southern and eastern Europe, Asia, the Caribbean, and Mexico—made the religious mix in America more and more complex. And the growth of cities allowed alternative religions to thrive.

At the same time many of the alternative religious movements that began in the nineteenth century or earlier continued their evolution into conventional denominations. Some exercised considerable religious and cultural influence, even though members of the mainline churches still regarded them as outsiders. The Quakers, for example, no longer engaged in radical prophetic activity. Yet they retained their religious commitment to peace and nonviolence, though their protests against war or the use of force took increasingly conventional forms of expression, such as political pressure. Similarly, the Seventh-day Adventists, still under the leadership of Ellen White at the turn of the century, no longer experienced the negative stigma associated with the Millerite movement from which they originated. On the contrary, by the turn of the century, the Adventist movement had moderated its apocalyptic message to the point where its members were very cautious about setting dates for the end of the world or Christ's return. They seemed preoccupied with building the institutions necessary for a long-term existence—schools, colleges, hospitals, and other church structures—none of which makes sense if the world is about to end tomorrow.

The Latter-day Saints, or Mormons, of all the earlier sects in the United States, made the greatest changes. In the 1860s the United States Army conducted military expeditions in

Mormon country searching for polygamists. In 1890 the church issued the Woodruff Manifesto, setting aside the practice of plural marriage. The Mormons showed themselves determined to do whatever was necessary to gain statehood for the Utah Territory. The quest for statehood apparently took precedence over the distinctive view of marriage that Joseph Smith, the founder, had established in a revelation. In 1896 Utah entered the Union as the forty-fifth state.

Christian Science at the turn of the century still enjoyed the leadership of its founder, Mary Baker Eddy, even though she had withdrawn from public activities. The success of the movement was manifest both in numbers and in the animosity the church and its leader aroused. Opposition to conventional medical practices set Christian Scientists apart from their neighbors, and on that issue they did not bend.

The most striking example of an alternative religion founded in the nineteenth century that retained its militant sectarian posture was Zion's Watch Tower Tract Society, later renamed the Jehovah's Witnesses. This group persisted in proclaiming impending destruction on the forces in American society opposed to Jehovah God, a coalition comprising churches, government, educational institutions, and the corporate world. Using biblical prophecy as the grounds for his calculation, Charles Taze Russell pointed ahead to the year 1914 as the likely moment of world destruction. The members of this movement proclaimed their apocalyptic message without apology or restraint.

With a few exceptions, therefore, the NRMs that began on the margins in earlier times were taking significant steps towards mainstream religious and social patterns in the United

States. Yet these groups often remained on the margins in the eyes of the members of the mainstream denominations.

Some NRMs that rose to prominence in urban settings, however, left little doubt about their place as outsiders. They stood out from their religious neighbors in various ways, including the fact that they were especially successful among African Americans.

The Peace Mission Movement originated in the New York City area. The founder was an African American, known to his followers as Father Divine. Mystery shrouds his early life. Divine probably was George Baker, born most likely in Maryland. It appears that he spent a number of years as the companion or partner of a traveling preacher who called himself Father Jehovia; Baker's self-designation was the Messenger. After several years together, when the two parted company, Baker, a.k.a. the Messenger, traveled widely, perhaps throughout the South, and maybe even to Azusa, preaching a message of the "possibilities" available to those who identified with God's spirit. In several places he came into conflict with the law. Eventually, like millions of other African Americans at the time, Baker migrated to the North, ending up in the New York City area.

The historical record becomes clearer in 1919 when we find a Major Jealous Divine (a.k.a. Baker, or the Messenger) living in a large house with his wife Peninniah in Sayville, Long Island. There they presided over a small community of followers to whom he offered assistance of several kinds: meals to those who were hungry, a place to sleep to those without a permanent residence, assistance in finding employment to those lacking a job, and a strong dose of positive thinking to those discouraged or depressed by their life situation. His followers participated in worship services at the house in Sayville. Divine's reputation slowly spread among members of the area's African-American community.

The increasing activity at Divine's house, however, caused rising concern among his neighbors. These were years in American history when racial conflict was widespread. Busloads of followers and the curious came on weekends to Sayville to be with Divine. He provided sumptuous feasts for those who attended the services. His followers took to calling him Reverend Divine or Father Divine. Within a few years the claims became even more exalted. Father Divine was declared by his followers to be God Almighty himself, and those who attended these meetings worshiped him. They sang his praises, and banners on the walls proclaimed his love and mercy.

A critical moment in the development of this sect came in the spring of 1931 when complaints about congestion in the neighborhood led to Divine's arrest for disturbing the peace. In an effort to reveal the racial motivations behind his arrest, Divine decided to go on trial rather than pay a fine. He was convicted and sentenced to a year in jail and a $500 fine by the judge, who had nothing but disdain for Divine and his "gullible" disciples. Four days later the judge suddenly died, and Father Divine was reported to have said in his jail cell, "I hated to do it." This episode and the stories circulating about him catapulted Divine into the public eye, especially within the African-American community, and set the stage for further expansion of his reputation. Divine was released from jail on appeal after three weeks.

In 1932 Father Divine moved the headquarters of his movement to Harlem. These were the most severe years of the Depression, when millions of Americans were out of work and

suffering extreme economic hardship. The Peace Mission
Movement soon spread from coast to coast by means of publications and the establishment of new sites, or colonies. The
movement was especially successful in New York and New
Jersey. Divine became a celebrity, and to his dedicated disciples
he was truly divine. He preached a message of hope and personal transformation in the face of extreme hardship.

Divine's proclamation about his own identity evolved further. He declared himself the Messiah promised in Old
Testament prophecies and the Second Coming of Christ
described in the New Testament. To his followers Father Divine
and his wife Mother Divine (Peninniah, or Sister Penny) person-
ified God as Father and Mother. His words they regarded as
revelation, and his writings as scripture. At banquets hymns
echoed Divine's praises:

Sing and Praise Him, Sing and Praise Him,
Sing and Praise Him for the Glorious Work He's Done.
Sing and Praise Him, Sing and Praise Him,
Glory Hallelujah for the Works He has done.

Divine provided his followers with food, shelter, consola-
tion, and hope; his converts gave him love and affection, praise
and thanksgiving, and all their earthly goods. They turned over
to him their money, property, wages, insurance policies—
everything they had. Father Divine, in turn, provided for all
their needs. In this respect the Peace Mission Movement was a
communitarian sect within the urban setting. Divine used the
collective resources to buy hotels, other property, and businesses in which his followers worked and which generated income
for the movement. He called the communal centers heavens
and his followers angels.

Those who accepted Father Divine entered a new world of his making. They took new names and obeyed a set of strict regulations governing the community. He demanded that his followers abstain from tobacco, alcohol, and profanity. In the heavens no marriages existed (except that of Father and Mother Divine), and no sexual relations were allowed. All became as brothers and sisters, even those who came into the movement as husband and wife. Men and women lived apart from one another. Divine required his followers to be honest, punctual, and hardworking. He forbade them to accept bribes or tips in their jobs. In the heavens, sickness, disease, and death received no public attention. No funerals were held to mourn the passing of members. Such problems were incompatible with the heavenly state.

Father Divine also addressed directly the racism of that day. Hatred often dominated relations between the races, and physical violence, including lynchings, against African Americans was commonplace. Divine declared all persons— black and white—equals. All were God's children, and therefore no racial distinctions were allowed. He forbade members of the community to use *black*, *white*, or *Negro* as racial terms. The word *peace* in the name of the movement was a specific reflection of his goal of racial harmony. Father Divine denounced the mob violence that was common at the time, and he affirmed his belief in the principle of equality expressed in the founding documents of the nation, including the Declaration of Independence.

As the years went by, the movement centered more and more attention on Father Divine himself. He presided over meetings and was the object of adoration and worship. He lived a lifestyle that set him apart from his followers in important ways. He owned an automobile and an airplane; he resided in a mansion on his Philadelphia estate called Woodmont, a location to which he had moved in 1942, when he lost a legal suit in New York state.

Sister Penny died sometime in 1943 without public notice. Three years later Father Divine married Sweet Angel, the new name of one of his personal secretaries, Edna Rose Ritchings, a white woman from Canada. Several months after their secret marriage Divine announced that Sweet Angel was the virginal reincarnation of Sister Penny. Divine's marriage to Sweet Angel, it appears, did not entail sexual relations.

In the years after the move to Philadelphia, the movement declined steadily. The improving economic conditions in America were one reason for that decline. In 1965 Father Divine died and was buried on the Woodmont estate. The second Mother Divine now presided over the movement, though the object of primary attention remained Father Divine's teachings. By the 1990s the community comprised only a few hundred members and the remaining properties and businesses.

The Peace Mission Movement was one of the first communities to be labeled a cult, in the negative sense of that term, by its critics and opponents.

Another NRM that began in this era, the Nation of Islam, emerged in a midwestern urban setting. It, too, had a measure of mystery surrounding its origins. In 1930 a mysterious silk peddler appeared in Detroit's ghetto proclaiming a very different religious message. His name was Wallace D. Fard (or Farrad), and he announced that he had come from the holy city of Mecca. He directed his message to the "so-called Negroes" of America. He challenged them to wake up and recognize their true identity. Fard declared that African Americans were, in truth, descendants of the Original Black Man, and that they were the superior race. Additionally, he told them that their true religion was Islam, not Christianity. Whenever Christianity had come to nonwhite peoples, he told them, it had been a religion of captivity and oppression. Islam—the proper religion of blacks—stood for freedom, justice, and equality.

Who was Fard, and where had he come from? That is where the mystery lies. Fard, who also had other names assigned to him, may have been influenced by Noble Drew Ali, founder of the Moorish Science Temple of America, a racially oriented variety of Islam. Drew Ali began his sect in the decade of World War I, drawing on ideas from both Islam and black nationalist, or black separatist, movements of the time. His group had some success in Detroit. Drew Ali died under mysterious circumstances, possibly even as the result of conflict among factions within the Moorish Science Temple. Fard may have been a close associate of Drew Ali.

The mystery surrounding Fard increased when, after achieving some considerable success in Detroit, he simply disappeared in 1934. But by that time he had established the ideology and structure for the Nation of Islam and had attracted to his movement several able converts whom he placed in positions of responsibility as the sect grew. Upon the disappearance of Fard, one of those lieutenants, Elijah Poole, whom Fard had renamed Elijah Muhammad, took over leadership of the movement. Fard had appointed him Minister of Islam and placed him in charge of the temple in Chicago. From that position Elijah Muhammad asserted control over the young sect. He

117

identified himself as the last messenger sent from God. Fard, he said, had been the Messiah, or Allah. Elijah Muhammad declared Fard's birthday in February to be Savior's Day, and the Black Muslims (as members of the Nation of Islam called themselves) celebrated it as a holiday. In the 1930s Elijah Muhammad consolidated his authority in the movement, clarified further its distinctive religious ideas, and strengthened its institutional structures.

Elijah Muhammad used his publications, including a newspaper entitled *Muhammad Speaks*, to recruit converts into the Nation of Islam. The core of this movement was its distinctive social theory concerning the different origins of the black and white races. According to Elijah Muhammad, the black race is descended from the Original Black Man. There was no known beginning of the black race; it has always been. The white race, by contrast, which he called a race of blue-eyed devils, is the product of a brilliant mad scientist named Yakub who had rebelled against Allah. Yakub, after being exiled to the Isle of Patmos as punishment, determined to continue his rebellion by creating a devil race. To accomplish this, over a period of several hundred years he genetically engineered a devil-like creature by a process of inbreeding. This new race, which was both physically and morally weaker than the black race, ended up as a white-skinned, stale-faced, blue-eyed monster, according to Elijah Muhammad. The white race was therefore Yakub's ultimate revenge.

This devil race was ultimately captured and placed in the caves of Europe from which it eventually escaped and rose to power, enslaving the black race in Africa. Whites also forced blacks to accept Christianity as their religion and to take white names. But Allah's ultimate plan has something else in store for both blacks and whites. In time, when the so-called Negroes recognize their true superiority and rise against their oppressors, then they will reclaim their rightful position. Blacks were encouraged to take *X* as a new surname as testimony that they had lost their own rightful names. Destruction—apocalyptic destruction—ultimately awaits white society, which has enslaved and oppressed blacks. Elijah Muhammad predicted the destruction of North America by fire—just retribution for the evils that whites have worked on blacks. The Nation of Islam proclaimed this dual message of captivity and redemption.

Elijah Muhammad established regulations governing nearly all aspects of life for the Black Muslims. He called for separation between the races. Blacks were to keep themselves untainted by avoiding interaction with whites. Blacks were to develop their own institutions—stores, schools, restaurants, farms, and ultimately their own nation. In this last regard Elijah Muhammad proposed that the United States set aside a portion of the nation's land—perhaps the Gulf coast states—to be turned into a black nation, separate from the United States. In this proposal he was echoing black nationalist sentiments expressed in earlier movements.

The Nation of Islam demanded that its members live a strict, almost puritanical, personal lifestyle. Elijah Muhammad condemned all premarital sexual activity as well as adultery. He forbade the eating of pork, a traditional Islamic prohibition, and cornbread because it was associated with the life of slavery and poverty. He also prohibited the use of liquor or drugs by Black Muslims. (It became standard procedure to check individuals when they entered the temple for worship.) He

119

instructed his followers to be punctual, hardworking, and responsible employees and to be thrifty. Elijah Muhammad placed a very positive emphasis on the importance of education for all members of the community, from the oldest to the youngest. The Black Muslims organized different educational activities for all age groups, from remedial instruction in rudimentary skills to African history, from classes in Arabic to practical homemaking.

Among their religious obligations, members of the Nation of Islam were to pray five times daily facing Mecca. Before each prayer they were ritually to cleanse the mouth as well as the hands, forearms, and feet. Black Muslims were required to attend at least two temple meetings per week. Yet this American sect did not subscribe to all of the standard requirements of traditional Islam, including the observance of the Ramadan fast; the duty of hajj, or pilgrimage to Mecca; and adherence to the Qur'an, or Koran, the scripture of orthodox Islam. On the contrary, the Bible seems to have functioned more importantly than the Qur'an for Black Muslims.

The Nation of Islam adopted a strong position on self-defense. Black Muslims were to stand up for their rights and defend themselves by force if necessary. One of the organizations founded by Fard and continued by Elijah Muhammad was named the Fruit of Islam, a paramilitary organization of young men in the community. They learned martial arts for the purpose of self-defense and in order that they might participate, if necessary, in the last great struggle between the forces of good and evil, the biblical Battle of Armageddon. In that mythic struggle, good would ultimately prevail.

The Nation of Islam came into greater prominence outside the African-American community in the 1960s, when Malcolm

X emerged as the most articulate spokesperson for the community. Malcolm converted to the Nation of Islam while in federal prison. He was totally committed to the cause and to the leadership of Elijah Muhammad until a series of incidents strained and finally broke that relationship. After a trip to Mecca and reevaluation of the views of the Black Muslims, Malcolm X broke with Elijah and formed his own more traditional Islamic organization, the Muslim Mosque, Inc. He also abandoned the racial ideology of the Nation of Islam in favor of orthodox Islam's principle of universal brotherhood. In 1965 Malcolm was murdered by members of the Nation of Islam. The years that followed were times of controversy for the tradition.

In the twentieth century cities came to symbolize both the promise and problems of the United States. In the urban centers were concentrations of wealth and poverty, grandeur and squalor, achievement and failure. Immigrants crowded into ethnic neighborhoods at the same time that African Americans from the South filled expanding ghettos. Political, social, and religious reformers struggled to improve conditions for those caught near the bottom of urban society, but those efforts had minimal impact. In these circumstances three NRMs involving African Americans—Pentecostalism, the Peace Mission Movement, and the Nation of Islam—arose. Each responded in different religious and social ways to the problems evident in cities.

Racially motivated violence was a fact of life for African Americans during the first half of the twentieth century. Race riots and lynchings of blacks were surprisingly common. Father Divine took a strong stand against racial distinctions and the violence generated by racial hatred. In this song sung by members of the Peace Mission Movement there is a vision of a United States free from such hatred, where brotherhood and love will reflect the spirit of the Bill of Rights.

Away down in Texas and in the farthest parts of the South
We shall eat and drink together, racism shall be wiped out.
There will be no more race riots and lynchings,
There will be no more division or strife
When they recognize God's Body, they will value each other's life.
Father will make them love each other so much with or without an antilynching bill
They will know that they are brothers and will not desire to kill.
Away down in Texas and in the farthest parts of the South
They will enact the Bill of Rights in every community,
Racialism shall be wiped out!

CHAPTER SEVEN

Twentieth-Century Sects and Cults

The 1960s was a decade of social, political, and religious turmoil, a time when many Americans celebrated the unconventional, the alternative, and the radical. Social unrest gave birth to the counterculture and hippie communes; political agitation fueled the Civil Rights movement and opposition to the war in Vietnam; religious ferment found expression in new interest in Eastern traditions and other spiritualities. The social, the political, and the religious were inseparable from one another.

Communes, for instance, featured both Eastern religious values and conservative Christian ideals. The International Society for Krishna Consciousness (ISKCON) is a notable example of the former; the Jesus People are a prominent case of the latter.

ISKCON emerged in the 1960s as a conspicuous and controversial NRM imported from the East. Swami Prabhupada founded this Hindu sect. A former businessman in India, he

123

gave up that vocation to devote himself to a life of service to the Hindu god Krishna, one of the most widely worshiped deities in that tradition. In 1965, at the age of sixty-nine, Prabhupada came to the United States and settled first in New York City, where he managed to attract a few disciples. Two years later he moved to San Francisco, where he established a new center. There the movement quickly became more successful, especially among young people who had been part of the counterculture. Prabhupada organized the society communally.

The most distinctive religious practice of the converts to ISKCON was chanting and dancing in public. Groups of devotees in saffron-colored robes with shaved heads chanted the sacred names of God:

Hare Krishna, Hare Krishna
Krishna Krishna, Hare Hare
Hare Rama, Hare Rama
Rama Rama, Hare Hare.

This activity attracted attention on the streets and provided members of the society an opportunity to distribute literature, recruit new converts, and solicit funds.

Prabhupada trained the converts in spiritual disciplines. They were to free themselves from concern with material things, sensory gratification, and the evils of the world. They were to devote themselves completely to the service of Krishna. Chanting and dancing in the streets had a function beyond fund-raising; it was also worship. Prabhupada invested the money raised in publishing facilities, in vegetarian food stores, and in real estate. These enterprises provided a solid economic base for the society.

Prabhupada also established rules of conduct for devotees. Members lived together in ashrams, or community houses. They ate no meat, fish, or eggs. If unmarried, they were not to engage in sexual relations. They were forbidden to use intoxicants or drugs, and they were not to gamble. Devotees submitted completely to Prabhupada as their spiritual master, but their primary task was to proclaim Krishna as their supreme lord.

Converts to ISKCON were also converts to Indian culture. Initiation into the society required that they break with their past and acquire a new identity. Male converts shaved their heads except for one lock and wore simple Indian-style clothing. Female converts dressed in saris, the traditional outer garment of a Hindu woman. Both men and women wore small beads around their necks as public acknowledgment of their devotion to Krishna. They also marked their bodies with clay markings to symbolize that they were temples of Krishna. They gave up their personal possessions. They adopted Indian ways of eating, bathing, and sleeping. After six months of following this routine, a member would receive a new name in recognition of a lifetime commitment to the service of Krishna.

By the mid-1970s there were fifty ISKCON temples throughout the United States with a total membership between four and five thousand. Prabhupada died in 1977, but the society under a board of directors managed to preserve the organization. They became, however, a favorite target of the anticult movement in the 1970s.

The Jesus People, also called the Jesus Movement, present a partial contrast to groups such as ISKCON. This movement, which also began in the 1960s, included hundreds of small

125

groups of Christians who often chose to live communally. These groups formed and disbanded without much public attention. Only rarely did one or another commune sustain itself for an extended period or become a permanent organization. The Jesus Movement therefore was highly diffuse and not organized around one leader or centered in one locality.

The small groups identified as Jesus People were generally committed to conservative Christian values. Many were explicitly evangelical and fundamentalist in outlook, evangelicals by their insistence on a conversion experience and fundamentalists by their conservative theological views. For instance, they regarded the Bible as their religious authority and were confident that they could interpret it correctly, without the guidance of clergy. They usually described, in highly emotional language, a personal relationship with Jesus as the religious experience at the center of the movement. Many who took part in the Jesus Movement were alienated from conventional religion and established churches. They frequently came into this movement after having been heavily involved in the counterculture. Their critics called them Jesus freaks and tended to lump them with other groups associated with the drug culture. They did share some interests with the counterculture, including a preference for unconventional clothing, long hair, and rock music.

The Jesus Movement sounded a mix of conservative religious themes and some radical social ideals. Many Jesus People expressed frustration with traditional forms of worship and searched for other ways to express their Christian faith. Apocalyptic interests attracted some of the young people who fell under the spell of such publications as Hal Lindsey's

The Late Great Planet Earth (1970), which predicted the impending destruction of the world. Others in the movement joined with those rebelling against technology, desiring a return to a simpler lifestyle.

As members of the Jesus Movement aged, they tended to lose the emotional zeal and religious energy that initially drove the movement. Only a few maintained distinctive communal patterns. Most of the Jesus People gradually moved back into more conventional religious groups.

The Unification Church was another imported sect that rose to prominence in the 1960s and attracted a great deal of negative attention. Formally the Holy Spirit Association for the Unification of World Christianity, adherents of this alternative religion were frequently identified as Moonies, a derogatory term derived from the name of the founder, the Reverend Sun Myung Moon, a native of North Korea, who converted to a Pentecostal form of Presbyterianism at the age of ten. Six years later he received a vision from Jesus Christ, as he reported, telling him that he was to restore the kingdom of God on earth. Following World War II he began a preaching career that led to more than ten years of imprisonment at the hands of the communists in North Korea. In 1957 after being released, he published a major text entitled *The Divine Principle*.

Moon asserted that he was locked in a personal struggle with Satan. He believed that he had been given special insight into God's plan for history. His mission was to reveal the future and convey insights that would lead to a better world. He affirmed that love was the controlling factor behind the creation of the world. But the first parents, Adam and Eve, misunderstood God's plan, misused love, and failed to establish the perfect family. Jesus' efforts to save the world were cut short by the crucifixion. Redemption is to come through a second Messiah who will restore and unify the global community through his marriage and the blessing of other marriages, thus bringing on the kingdom of God on earth. The Reverend Moon, according to the Unification Church, is that Messiah.

From its initial appearance in the United States, the Unification Church has been a favorite object of attack by anticult forces. The aggressive solicitation of funds by members was one source of this hostility. Moon's conservative political agenda has been another cause of contention. The extensive financial interests of the church have also brought criticism. In 1984 Moon was convicted of income tax evasion and sentenced to prison, where he spent thirteen months. Even more negative publicity has focused on the interracial group marriages over which Moon and his wife have presided.

Although the Unification Church has been a favorite target of critics and anticult groups, Moon has consistently supported a number of movements that enjoy widespread popularity in the United States. For example, the organization is aggressively patriotic and vocally anticommunist. It has spent large sums of money on behalf of pro-family activities, the anti-abortion movement, the support of religious freedom, and the national effort to establish conservative Christian schools as an alternative to public schools. It is estimated that by the 1980s membership in the United States was more than five thousand.

In the 1960s the Church of Scientology, another alternative religious movement that began somewhat earlier, also attracted growing attention and increasing hostility from critics. This new religion was founded by L. Ron Hubbard, a widely traveled writer with interests in science fiction, who was wounded while serving in the Navy during the Second World War. He spent time developing a system of unique ideas, writing drafts, and finally in 1950 publishing his religious and theological views as a book entitled *Dianetics: The Modern Science of Mental Health*. Hubbard claimed that the concepts described in *Dianetics* constituted a "science of mind" and offered a therapy and cure for mental illness and other psychosomatic problems. Hubbard's system involved his own distinctive blend of religious, scientific, and psychological thought. He also began quickly to establish a series of organizations devoted to research and promotion of his ideas. *Dianetics* caught on among those interested in science fiction as well as in alternative therapies, and in 1951 it was a national best-seller. Two years later the Church of Scientology was formally incorporated.

Hubbard's ideas are not easily summarized. Although fundamentally optimistic about the goodness of people, Scientology is designed to assist individuals' escape from the limits of the present state, a problem caused by the destructive force of the "reactive mind." The true self, what Hubbard labeled the Thetan, will be freed when unconscious memories, called engrams, are brought to the surface by a therapeutic process called auditing. When individuals reflect on the engrams and restore rational thought and behavior, they will enjoy wholeness and happiness. This summary does not do justice to the complexity of Hubbard's ideas, which additionally involve a series of stages through which Scientologists move as they progress from the dominance of the reactive mind to full control, a condition Hubbard called clear.

One of the unique devices employed to assist in this spiritual or psychological passage is the E-Meter, a machine resembling a lie detector that records emotional reactions to words and therefore, according to Hubbard, measures the state of the individual's well-being. An auditor administers the process and serves in some sense as a technological therapist and spiritual counselor. The goal of being clear means for members freedom from psychological stress and physical pain. Hubbard combined these distinctive beliefs and practices with other unusual notions concerning the ability of individuals as spirits to operate outside their bodies and the ultimate prospect that individuals might rise above all limitations imposed on them through the physical body over the course of many lifetimes and almost endless years. Many of these more advanced ideas are not widely discussed by members of the community.

Scientology bears the marks of its founder's interests in science fiction, imaginative writing, psychological theory, and religion. Critics and members alike are not always sure how best to categorize it. It is possible to be a member of the Church of Scientology and remain affiliated with another religious community.

Hubbard's ideas have been a favorite target of critics, and the Church of Scientology has been the object of sustained anticult activity, especially in recent decades. Critics have accused Hubbard of making bogus claims concerning the psychological and physical benefits of the auditing process. The federal government's Food and Drug Administration has seized E-Meters, charging that they were being used inappropriately in the diagnosis of illness. The Internal Revenue Service has had unending conflict with the Church of Scientology, at one point revoking its tax-exempt status. Individuals have repeatedly filed lawsuits against the church, claiming that they were duped out of large sums of money that they paid for auditing. Members of the church have been convicted on charges of theft of government documents. And most recently, the German government has lodged charges against the church for abuse of its members and for being too controlling.

This opposition and these controversies have not slowed the expansion of the church; nor did the death of Hubbard in 1986 bring the community to an end. At this writing there are more than seven hundred local branch churches affiliated with the Church of Scientology, which has its headquarters in Los Angeles. Scientologists, in fact, have turned some of this negative publicity to the church's advantage, having launched a very sophisticated and seemingly successful public relations effort on its behalf. The anticult movement, however, continues to identify Scientology as one of its primary targets.

Sects and cults often pass through stages, sometimes moving away from radical dissent toward accommodation of the dominant society. Two examples from recent decades illustrate this mainstreaming process.

Transcendental Meditation (TM), a NRM that arrived in the United States in 1959, led by the thin, bearded, white-robed guru, or religious teacher, Maharishi Mahesh Yogi, provides one example of the evolution of a sect. TM began as a religious movement based on ancient Hindu patterns of spirituality. Transcendental Meditation, like a number of other Eastern traditions, featured the use of a *mantra*, "a sacred tone, word, or phrase," as a tool for meditation and edification.

On arrival in the United States, Maharishi became an instant celebrity. This diminutive Eastern master, who twirled long-stemmed roses and giggled at times like a child, brought the East, exotic to Americans with its incense and foreign terminology, into the living rooms of middle America. He appeared on television talk shows and in the news magazines. For a time his entourage included the Beatles.

Ten years or so after its arrival in the United States, TM began to change its public image by dropping its explicit links to Hindu spirituality and promoting itself as a meditation technique with measurable psychological and physiological benefits. Its advocates appealed to scientific data, including biofeedback, rather than to spiritual benefits, in urging its adoption. In the mid-1970s the movement founded Maharishi International University in Fairfield, Iowa, an institution that granted conventional college degrees as well as a Ph.D. in the neuroscience of human consciousness. TM soon faded from the public eye, for it was no longer the threatening cult it had once seemed. Now it took its place among competing therapeutic enterprises.

The Nation of Islam has also gone through a process of dramatic mainstreaming in recent decades. When Elijah Muhammad died in 1975, his son Wallace D. Muhammad took over leadership. Within a very short time he changed the fundamental orientation of the movement. He began by disavowing the racial ideology that had served as the basis for the distinctive claims of the Black Muslims regarding the superiority of the black race and the inferiority of the white race. This change was informed by his intention to move the sect toward traditional Islam. Wallace D. Muhammad recognized what Malcolm X had perceived earlier, namely, that the Nation of Islam was badly out of step with traditional Islam. He intended to alter that situation. Wallace D. Muhammad "de-deified" blacks and "de-demonized" whites in the process. He placed a new emphasis

on the Holy Qur'an and on the traditional religious responsibilities of an orthodox Muslim. He changed the name of the
movement to the American Muslim Mission, and then later formally dissolved it as a national entity. He entered the public
arena in a way that his father never had, speaking out on political and social issues. He no longer condemned the national
government, nor did he call for a separate black nation.

These changes were dramatic and controversial, so much so
that some members of the organization were unwilling to continue under Muhammad's leadership. These circumstances gave
rise to the emergence of Louis Farrakhan in the late 1970s.
Farrakhan, who was the leader of the Harlem mosque where
Malcolm X had once presided, separated from the American
Muslim Mission and set about reconstituting the Nation of
Islam as it had been under Elijah Muhammad. In subsequent
years he has seized the headlines with his inflammatory rhetoric
and activism. In the case of the Black Muslims, the mainstreaming process has produced one new organization intent on
assimilating to orthodox Islam and one rejuvenated organization intent on returning to earlier radical dissenting patterns.

Public controversy continues to surround alternative religions in the United States. Three tragic events in the late
twentieth century have underscored the general lack of understanding of sects and cults. The three cases that have received
massive media attention are the suicide/murders in 1978 of Jim
Jones and his followers, the fiery inferno in 1993 that destroyed
David Koresh and his community, and the group suicide in
1997 led by Marshall Herff Applewhite. These three tragedies,
the media coverage of them, and the flood of commentary have
left an indelibly negative impression of sects and cults on the

public consciousness. Each of the three groups fits the dissenting patterns that have been observed in NRMs.

Jim Jones, a native of Indiana and an ordained minister in the Disciples of Christ denomination, first gathered an interracial congregation in Indianapolis, where he was a vigorous advocate for social and racial justice. When he led that community to California, they attracted even more members and gained a reputation for supporting liberal causes. Problems, however, developed for Jones in that location, and as a result he and his followers left the United States and settled in the jungles of Guyana in South America. There in 1974 they began building a socialist community called Jonestown, where Jones's actions and ideas became irrational and paranoid. He exercised dictatorial control over the lives of his followers, engaged in deviant sexual practices with members of the community, and was abusive in other ways. He created a climate of fear, making his followers believe that they might be attacked suddenly by agents of the U.S. government. He became unbalanced mentally and possibly was on drugs.

The end of the Peoples Temple and the tragic suicide/ murder of more than nine hundred persons in Guyana followed a visit by a United States congressman whom they murdered. Jones then persuaded or forced the members of the community to commit suicide by drinking poison-laced Kool-Aid.

The response to the discovery of this tragedy by journalists, clergy, politicians, and the general public in the United States was horror and a desire to distance themselves from the events at Jonestown. No one wanted to be tainted by association with this cult. Public figures who commented on the tragedy showed surprisingly little understanding of such dissenting groups. Jonestown provided fuel for the anticult campaign.

David Koresh came on the scene at Mount Carmel, outside
Waco, Texas, many years after that community had first been
formed. The Branch Davidians, as the sect called itself, was an
offshoot of the Seventh-day Adventist Church. The Waco community began a separate existence in 1934 under the leadership
of a dissident Adventist named Victor Houteff, who, along with
his followers, established Mount Carmel with the expectation
that they would play a special role in the Second Coming of
Christ, which was about to occur. A series of leadership changes
and conflicts within the community preceded Koresh's arrival.
Koresh, born Vernon Howell, came to Mount Carmel in 1981.
He soon became involved in yet another power struggle in the
group and by late 1987 had taken control of the community
with the support of one faction.

The Branch Davidians expected Christ's speedy return.
They worshiped on Saturdays and maintained a number of
strict behavioral requirements. They did not eat meat or use
alcohol or tobacco; they avoided worldly entanglements, such
as fancy clothing and watching television. Howell, who
changed his name to Koresh in 1990, believed he had a messianic role to play. He was to "open," or interpret, the Seven
Seals of the book of Revelation. He was also to raise up a special lineage of God's children, and therefore he considered the
women at Mount Carmel his spiritual wives.

The tragic end of Mount Carmel was triggered by an
abortive raid by federal agents of the Bureau of Alcohol,
Tobacco, and Firearms, who were serving warrants relating to
weapons charges. The Branch Davidians bought and sold
firearms at gun shows as a source of income. In that raid four
agents and six Davidians were killed by gunfire. The resulting
fifty-one-day standoff between law enforcement officers and

the community ended when the government infiltrated the compound with tear gas in the hope of ending the siege. Fire broke out, and another seventy-four Branch Davidians, including women, children, and Koresh, died in the ensuing inferno.

A wave of recriminations followed. Critics, law enforcement officers, the few Davidians who survived the ordeal, outside observers, and federal officials exchanged charges and countercharges. No one stepped up to take responsibility for the tragedy. Again this episode evoked a chorus of negative judgments about sects and cults and a new wave of anticult sentiment.

In the 1970s Marshall Herff Applewhite and Bonnie Nettles cofounded a UFO cult in California. Known as Bo and Peep, Do and Ti, and Tiddly and Wink, the Two, as they referred to themselves, led a small community of believers in a cult focusing on a religious interpretation of unidentified flying objects piloted by extraterrestrial beings or visitors. Public interest in UFOs dates from the period following World War II. The rise of the Space Age and the growth of science fiction fed this interest, generating, among other things, a new vocabulary. Debates ensued about the nature of extraterrestrials. Were they demonic or salvific? Were they destructive or redemptive?

Applewhite was the son of a Presbyterian minister; Nettles was very interested in astrology. They shared an interest in searching for a higher life. One name they gave their movement was Human Individual Metamorphosis (HIM). They expected at one point to be killed, subsequently resurrected, and then carried off by a UFO into outer space where they would find the "Father's kingdom." Applewhite and Nettles used the transformation of a lowly caterpillar emerging from a cocoon as a beautiful butterfly as an image of the metamorphosis they expected to undergo upon boarding the UFO. They were joined by a group of fellow travelers who also desired something beyond their present existence. For several years this group stayed out of the public eye, spending long periods in isolation in the wilderness.

After the death of Nettles in 1985, Applewhite changed his strategy, and this UFO cult eventually became centered in San Diego, where members established a computer consulting firm. They lived communally and cut themselves off from all association with their biological families as part of their effort to sever human ties. They renounced all addictions to alcohol, drugs, or tobacco. Similarly, they abstained from all sexual relations. In fact, after the group suicide it was discovered that several members of the community had undergone castration.

In the spring of 1997, thirty-nine members of this community, under the leadership of Applewhite, committed a collective, ritualized, almost sanitized group suicide, using an applesauce cocktail laced with poison. The members of Heaven's Gate, another name for the movement, dressed in similar clothing and stretched out on their beds in an orderly manner. They left videotapes explaining their actions. The timing of their action was triggered by their conviction that following in the tail of the Hale-Bopp comet was a spacecraft that was coming to pick them up. They planned to travel by this means to "the Level Above Human."

The community's Web site included the following statement:

Whether Hale-Bopp has a "companion" or not is
 irrelevant from our perspective. However, its arrival is
 joyously very significant to us at "Heaven's Gate." The
 joy is that our Older Member in the Evolutionary Level

Above Human (the Kingdom of Heaven) has made it
clear to us that Hale-Bopp's approach is the "marker"
we've been waiting for—the time for the arrival of the
spacecraft from the Level Above Human to take us
home to "Their World"—in the literal Heavens.

The events of spring 1997 triggered yet another outcry
against sects and cults. Jonestown, Waco, and Heaven's Gate
seemed to confirm the widespread public perception that all
outsider religious groups are weird, bizarre, unbalanced, radical, and ultimately dangerous. That is untrue. It is, of course,
unfortunate that these tragedies occurred. At the same time,
however, it is also unfortunate that so little effort has been
made to understand New Religious Movements. These recent
tragedies are rare exceptions when we consider the number of
alternative religions that have functioned positively for their
members and society.

By this point the pattern is clear. In every period of the
history of the United States sects and cults have increased the
number and diversity of religious options available. The
United States has been a fertile seedbed for the growth of
NRMs. One historian writing about this pattern has described
the religious environment of the nineteenth century as a spiritual hothouse, a designation that might apply almost as well to
all periods of U.S. history.

Outsider religious traditions have functioned positively in
the lives of hundreds of thousands of Americans. These sects
and cults provide their members coherent ways to find meaning in life, organize relationships, structure ethical and ritual
systems, and affirm the existence of transcendent realities.
These are the same functions that every religion addresses.

Alternative religions provide their adherents alternative ways to be religious.

In the United States sects and cults also assist in keeping the constitutional system honest. The First Amendment prohibits the legal establishment of any particular religion and guarantees the free exercise of all faiths. The former principle of disestablishment restricts the government from supporting one or more religious traditions through tax revenues or by any form of constraint, such as law enforcement. The latter principle of free exercise affirms equal rights for all people to practice their religious activities, no matter what the specifics of their beliefs are. Adoption of the First Amendment to the Constitution was a truly remarkable decision by the founders of our nation. These constitutional principles were not commonplace in the eighteenth century. But both principles are also potentially subject to being subverted in one way or another.

For instance, if a few powerful religious denominations become overwhelmingly dominant in American society, they may constitute a kind of informal religious establishment by virtue of their power and numbers. It could be difficult for those citizens who are not members of these denominations to oppose them publicly on ethical, social, political, or cultural issues. The presence of many different—indeed, very different—religious groups in the United States is one possible safeguard against the development of an unofficial religious establishment.

Similarly, the principle of free exercise is potentially subject to subversion. For example, if a few powerful religious denominations decide that acceptable religious activity excludes spiritual practices and behavior different from their own, the principle of religious freedom may be severely constrained. The free exercise of religion could be limited to a narrow set of options. Sects and cults in the United States, engaging in highly diverse religious activities, are a possible check on the impulse to narrow the range of free exercise and a reminder of the potential breadth of the principle.

Alternative religions in the United States have helped to keep our constitutional system honest during the second half of the twentieth century, a time that has witnessed accelerating religious pluralism. Pluralism is a key concept for understanding American religion. *Plural*, of course, means "more than one." *Religious pluralism* is the term that identifies the American system as accommodating more than one religious tradition. The history of the nation's alternative religions is a critical part of the story of its religious pluralism.

Ideally, social peace and harmony would accompany the growth of religious pluralism in the United States. But, unfortunately, conflict, hatred, and hostility more frequently mark relations between religious insiders and outsiders, and even relations among various outsider groups. Tragically, the pattern of animosity does not seem to be lessening. On the contrary, the level of antagonism toward sects and cults since the 1970s seems to have escalated.

Anticult organizations, such as the Cult Awareness Network, rose to prominence in the 1970s and 1980s. The announced purpose of these groups is to combat the influence of sects and cults by disseminating hostile literature about them; persuading members of these groups to leave, sometimes by force; attempting to deprogram members; and filing civil suits in the courts against these organizations in order to gain custody of family members or control their financial assets. The anticult movement is itself highly controversial. Some defend it as a watchdog organization designed to protect individuals from religious entrapment. Others criticize it as a gross violation of individual rights, including free exercise of religion.

For several decades it has been fashionable to suggest that the United States is becoming an increasingly secular society. *Secular*, in this sense, means "the opposite of religious." The corollary of that judgment is that religion is losing its importance. This secularization theory gained widespread support among academics, the clergy, cultural observers, and the general public.

But evidence from the closing decades of the twentieth century does not confirm all parts of this theory. Religion is not disappearing from our nation. On the contrary, institutional religious activity is thriving in the United States, and personal religious commitment remains important for the majority of Americans. One convincing piece of evidence against the secularization theory is the continuing, if not expanding, vitality of alternative religions. These outsider groups—although hated, ridiculed, and even persecuted—continue to attract many adherents and contribute substantially to the vitality and creativity of the nation's religious life.

In fact, alternative religions constitute perhaps the most innovative, creative, and productive portion of the religious scene in the contemporary United States. Understanding NRMs is important because it is certain that the United States will continue to be home to many alternative religious communities in the future.

NRMs often used the language and ideas of traditional Christianity in different and distinctive ways, thereby incurring the special opposition of mainstream churches. The Unification Church developed a unique view of the messianic roles of Jesus and the Reverend Moon. On February 3, 1977, Frederick Sontag, who was writing a book about the Unification Church, asked Moon the following question: "How do you see your own role in relation to the role of Jesus?" Here is Moon's answer.

One of my most important revelations is that Jesus Christ did not come to die. He came to this world to consummate his messianic mission given by God, which is the establishment of the kingdom of God here on earth. Through his crucifixion, however, Jesus gave himself as a sacrifice for the faithlessness of the world, and by his resurrection, he established spiritual salvation. This is the teaching of the *Divine Principle*. Complete salvation, which is physical as well as spiritual, was the ultimate purpose and intended goal of God for mankind at the time of Jesus. That mission was not totally accomplished. We must realize, however, that this was not because of any fault on the part of Jesus Christ. Rather it was because of the rejection by the people. This point is greatly misunderstood. The Second Coming was predicted because the mission was not totally accomplished in the first. Therefore, a messianic crusade is destined to begin here on earth in order to consummate the will of

God. The work of the Unification Church and my mission is to proclaim the coming of the Messianic Age.

From the Christian church's point of view, my teaching, the new revelation, is not only extraordinary, but revolutionary. I can understand why Christians call us heretics. But most important, who will God call a heretic? From God's point of view, my revelation is deeply orthodox. If the mission of Jesus Christ had been completely fulfilled in his time, then there would be no need for the birth of the Unification Church. My mission would not be needed.

CHRONOLOGY

1635
Roger Williams banished from Massachusetts Bay Colony

1638
Anne Hutchinson tried before the Church in Boston

1647
George Fox proclaims the Quaker message in England

1682
William Penn arrives in America to found Pennsylvania

1683
Mennonites settle in Germantown, Pennsylvania

1692
Witch trials in Salem, Massachusetts

1732
Conrad Beissel founds the Ephrata Community in Pennsylvania

1774
Ann Lee and English Shakers arrive in New York City

1791
First Amendment to United States Constitution ratified

1803
George Rapp comes to United States from Germany

1817–19
The Vermont Pilgrims, led by Isaac Bullard, make their westward journey

1841
Brook Farm founded by George Ripley in West Roxbury, Massachusetts

1844
The Millerite Great Disappointment

1848
Rappings begin in the Fox home in Hydesville, New York

1848
John Humphrey Noyes founds Oneida in central New York

1863
Ellen White and others organize the Seventh-day Adventist Church

1869
Charles Taze Russell organizes a Bible study group

1875
Mary Baker Eddy publishes *Science and Health*

1875
Helena P. Blavatsky and Henry S. Olcott found the Theosophical Society

1897
Katherine Tingley establishes Point Loma in San Diego, California

1906
Azusa Street revival begins in Los Angeles under William Seymour

1919
Father Divine begins activities in Sayville, Long Island

1930
Wallace D. Fard initiates the Nation of Islam in Detroit, Michigan

1959
Maharishi Mahesh Yogi brings Transcendental Meditation to America

1965
Swami Prabhupada arrives in United States from India

1975
Elijah Muhammad dies; his son Wallace D. Muhammad succeeds him as leader of the Nation of Islam

1978
Suicide/murders of Jim Jones and the Peoples Temple in Guyana

1993
Destruction of David Koresh and the Branch Davidians at Waco, Texas

1996
Bankrupt Cult Awareness Network now controlled by Church of Scientology

1997
Group suicide of Heaven's Gate members led by Marshall Herff Applewhite

2000
Controversial Danforth Report on Waco exonerates government officials from ultimate responsibility for the disaster

FURTHER READING

GENERAL READING ON RELIGION IN THE UNITED STATES

Albanese, Catherine L. *America: Religions and Religion.* Rev. ed. Belmont, Calif.: Wadsworth, 1992.

Ahlstrom, Sydney E. *A Religious History of the American People.* New Haven: Yale University Press, 1972.

Bonomi, Patricia U. *Under the Cope of Heaven: Religion, Society, and Politics in Colonial America.* New York: Oxford University Press, 1986.

Butler, Jon. *Awash in a Sea of Faith: Christianizing the American People.* Cambridge: Harvard University Press, 1990.

Butler, Jon, and Harry S. Stout, eds. *Religion in American History: A Reader.* New York: Oxford University Press, 1997.

Gaustad, Edwin S. *A Religious History of America.* Rev. ed. San Francisco: Harper & Row, 1990.

Marty, Martin E. *Pilgrims in Their Own Land: 500 Years of Religion in America.* New York: Penguin, 1985.

McDannell, Colleen, ed. *Religions of the United States in Practice.* 2 vols. Princeton: Princeton University Press, 2001.

Tweed, Thomas A., ed. *Retelling U.S. Religious History.* Berkeley: University of California Press, 1997.

Williams, Peter W. *America's Religions: From Their Origins to the Twenty-First Century.* Urbana: University of Illinois Press, 2002.

DISSENTING RELIGIOUS COMMUNITIES IN GENERAL

Barker, Eileen. *New Religious Movements.* London: Her Majesty's Stationary Office, 1989.

Bednarowski, Mary Farrell. *New Religions and the Theological Imagination in America.* Bloomington: Indiana University Press, 1989.

Bestor, Arthur. *Backwoods Utopias.* Philadelphia: University of Pennsylvania Press, 1950.

Bloom, Harold. *The American Religion: The Emergence of the Post-Christian Nation.* New York: Simon & Schuster, 1992.

Boyer, Paul. *When Time Shall Be No More: Prophecy Belief in Modern American Culture.* Cambridge: Harvard University Press, 1992.

Braden, Charles S. *These Also Believe.* New York: Macmillan, 1949.

Chmielewski, Wendy E., Louis J. Kern, and Marlyn Klee-Hartzell, eds. *Women in Spiritual and Communitarian Societies in the United States.* Syracuse: Syracuse University Press, 1993.

Conkin, Paul K. *American Originals: Homemade Varieties of Christianity.* Chapel Hill: University of North Carolina Press, 1997.

Dawson, Lorne L. *Comprehending Cults: The Sociology of New Religious Movements.* Toronto: Oxford University Press, 1998.

Ellwood, Robert S. *Alternative Altars: Unconventional and Eastern Spirituality in America.* Chicago: University of Chicago Press, 1979.

Ellwood, Robert S., and Harry B. Partin. *Religious and Spiritual Groups in Modern America.* Engelwood Cliffs, N.J.: Prentice Hall, 1988.

Fogarty, Robert S. *All Things New: American Communes and Utopian Movements, 1860–1914.* Chicago: University of Chicago Press, 1990.

_____. *Dictionary of American Communal and Utopian History*. Westport, Conn.: Greenwood Press, 1980.

Foster, Lawrence. *Women, Family, and Utopia: Communal Experiments of the Shakers, the Oneida Community, and the Mormons*. Syracuse: Syracuse University Press, 1991.

Fuller, Robert C. *Alternative Medicine and American Religious Life*. New York: Oxford University Press, 1989.

Godbeer, Richard. *The Devil's Dominion: Magic and Religion in Early New England*. New York: Cambridge University Press, 1992.

Gura, Philip F. *A Glimpse of Sion's Glory: Puritan Radicalism in New England, 1620–1660*. Middletown, Conn.: Wesleyan University Press, 1984.

Jenkins, Philip. *Mystics and Messiahs: Cults and New Religions in American History*. New York: Oxford University Press, 2000.

Kerr, Howard, and Charles L. Crow, eds. *The Occult in America: New Historical Perspectives*. Urbana: University of Illinois Press, 1983.

Lewis, James R., ed. *Odd Gods: New Religions & the Cult Controversy*. Amherst, N.Y.: Prometheus Books, 2001.

_____. *The Gods Have Landed: New Religions from Other Worlds*. Albany: State University of New York Press, 1995.

Lovejoy, David S. *Religious Enthusiasm in the New World: Heresy to Revolution*. Cambridge: Harvard University Press, 1985.

Marini, Stephen A. *Radical Sects of Revolutionary New England*. Cambridge: Harvard University Press, 1982.

McLoughlin, William G. *New England Dissent, 1630–1833*. 2 vols. Cambridge: Harvard University Press, 1971.

Melton, J. Gordon. *The Encyclopedia of American Religions*. 4th ed. Detroit: Gale Research, 1986.

_____. *Encyclopedic Handbook of Cults in America*. Rev. ed. New York: Garland, 1992.

Miller, Timothy, ed. *America's Alternative Religions*. Albany: State University of New York Press, 1995.

Moore, R. Laurence. *Religious Outsiders and the Making of Americans*. New York: Oxford University Press, 1986.

Muncy, Raymond Lee. *Sex and Marriage in Utopian Communities: 19th-Century America*. Bloomington: Indiana University Press, 1973.

Peel, Robert. *Spiritual Healing in a Scientific Age*. San Francisco: Harper & Row, 1987.

Pitzer, Donald E., ed. *America's Communal Utopias*. Chapel Hill: University of North Carolina Press, 1997.

Saliba, John A. *Understanding New Religious Movements*. Grand Rapids: Eerdmans, 1995.

Sarna, Jonathan D., ed. *Minority Faiths and the American Protestant Mainstream*. Urbana: University of Illinois Press, 1998.

Spann, Edward K. *Brotherly Tomorrows: Movements for a Cooperative Society in America 1820–1920*. New York: Columbia University Press, 1989.

Weisman, Richard. *Witchcraft, Magic, and Religion in 17th-Century Massachusetts*. Amherst: University of Massachusetts Press, 1984.

Wessinger, Catherine, ed. *Women's Leadership in Marginal Religions: Explorations Outside the Mainstream*. Urbana: University of Illinois Press, 1993.

SPECIFIC DISSENTING RELIGIOUS COMMUNITIES

Allen, James B., and Glen M. Leonard. *The Story of the Latter-day Saints*. Salt Lake City: Deseret Book Company, 1992.

Anderson, Robert Mapes. *Vision of the Disinherited: The Making of American Pentecostalism*. New York: Oxford University Press, 1979.

Arrington, Leonard J., and Davis Bitton. *The Mormon Experience: A History of the Latter-day Saints*. New York: Knopf, 1979.

Barbour, Hugh, and J. William Frost, ed. *The Quakers.* New York: Greenwood, 1988.

Barthel, Diane L. *Amana: From Pietist Sect to American Community.* Lincoln: University of Nebraska Press, 1984.

Blumhofer, Edith L. *Restoring the Faith: The Assemblies of God, Pentecostalism, and American Culture.* Urbana: University of Illinois Press, 1993.

Bowman, Carol E. *Brethren Society: The Cultural Transformation of a Peculiar People.* Baltimore: Johns Hopkins University Press, 1995.

Boyer, Paul, and Stephen Nissenbaum. *Salem Possessed: The Social Origins of Witchcraft.* Cambridge: Harvard University Press, 1974.

Brandon, George. *Santeria from Africa to the New World.* Bloomington: Indiana University Press, 1993.

Braude, Ann. *Radical Spirits: Spiritualism and Women's Rights in Nineteenth-Century America.* Boston: Beacon Press, 1989.

Bromley, David. G., and Anson D. Shupe, Jr. *Moonies in America: Cult, Church, Crusade.* Beverly Hills, Calif.: Sage, 1979.

Bromley, David G., and Larry D. Shinn, eds. *Krishna Consciousness in the West.* Lewisburg, Penn.: Bucknell University Press, 1989.

Brown, Karen McCarthy. *Mama Lola: A Vodou Priestess in Brooklyn.* Berkeley: University of California Press, 1991.

Butler, Jon. *The Huguenots in America.* Cambridge: Harvard University Press, 1983.

Campbell, Bruce F. *Ancient Wisdom Revived: A History of the Theosophical Movement.* Berkeley: University of California Press, 1980.

Carroll, Bret E. *Spiritualism in Antebellum America.* Bloomington: Indiana University Press, 1997.

Chidester, David. *Salvation and Suicide: An Interpretation of Jim Jones, the Peoples Temple, and Jonestown.* Bloomington: Indiana University Press, 1988.

Chryssides, George D. *The Advent of Sun Myung Moon: The Origins, Beliefs, and Practices of the Unification Church.* New York: St. Martin's, 1991.

Covington, Dennis. *Salvation on Sand Mountain: Snake Handling and Redemption in Southern Appalachia.* New York: Penguin Books, 1995.

Curtis, Edward E., IV. *Islam in Black America: Identity, Liberation, and Difference in African-American Islamic Thought.* Albany: State University of New York Press, 2002.

Davies, Douglas J. *The Mormon Culture of Salvation: Force, Grace, and Glory.* Burlington, Vt.: Ashgate Publishing, 2000.

Dayton, Donald W. *Theological Roots of Pentecostalism.* Grand Rapids: Zondervan, 1987.

Dyck, Cornelius J. *An Introduction to Mennonite History: A Popular History of the Anabaptists and the Mennonites.* Scottdale, Penn.: Herald Press, 1981.

Elmen, Paul. *Wheat Flour Messiah: Eric Jansson of Bishop Hill.* Carbondale, Ill.: Southern Illinois University Press, 1976.

Fauset, Arthur Huff. *Black Gods of the Metropolis.* Philadelphia: University of Pennsylvania Press, 1944.

Gardell, Mattias. *In the Name of Elijah Muhammad: Louis Farrakhan and the Nation of Islam.* Durham, N.C.: Duke University Press, 1996.

Gaustad, Edwin Scott. *The Rise of Adventism: Religion and Society in Mid-Nineteenth-Century America.* New York: Harper & Row, 1974.

Gottschalk, Stephen. *The Emergence of Christian Science in American Religious Life.* Berkeley: University of California Press, 1973.

Hall, David D. *Witch-Hunting in Seventeenth-Century New England: A Documentary History.* Boston: Northeastern University Press, 1991.

Hall, John R. *Gone from the Promised Land: Jonestown in American Cultural History.* New Brunswick, N.J.: Transaction, 1987.

Hamm, Thomas D. *The Transformation of American Quakerism: Orthodox Friends, 1800–1907*. Bloomington: Indiana University Press, 1988.

Harris, Lis. *Holy Days: The World of a Hasidic Family*. New York: Summit Books, 1985.

Harvey, Graham. *Contemporary Paganism: Listening People Speaking Earth*. New York: New York University Press,1997.

Hostetler, John A. *Amish Society*. Rev. ed. Baltimore: The Johns Hopkins Press, 1968.

Jackson, Carl T. *Vedanta for the West: The Ramakrishna Movement in the United States*. Bloomington: Indiana University Press, 1994.

Judah, J. Stillson. *The History and Philosophy of Metaphysical Movements in America*. Philadelphia: Westminster Press, 1967.

Karlsen, Carol F. *The Devil in the Shape of a Woman: Witchcraft in Colonial New England*. New York: Norton, 1987.

Kimbrough, David L. *Taking Up Serpents: Snake Handlers of Eastern Kentucky*. Chapel Hill: University of North Carolina Press, 1995.

Klaw, Spencer. *Without Sin: The Life and Death of the Oneida Community*. New York: Allen Lane, 1993.

Kraybill, Donald B. *The Riddle of Amish Culture*. Baltimore: Johns Hopkins University Press, 1989.

Land, Gary, ed. *Adventism in America: A History*. Grand Rapids: Eerdmans, 1986.

Lewis, James R. *From the Ashes: Making Sense of Waco*. Lanham, Md.: Rowman & Littlefield, 1994.

Lewis, William F. *Soul Rebels: The Rastafari*. Prospect Heights, Ill.: Waveland, 1993.

Lincoln, C. Eric. *The Black Muslims in America*. Boston: Beacon Press, 1961.

Lucas, Phillip Charles. *The Odyssey of a New Religion: The Holy Order of MANS from New Age to Orthodoxy*. Bloomington: Indiana University Press, 1995.

MacMaster, Richard K. *Land, Piety, Peoplehood: The Establishment of Mennonite Communities in America 1683–1790*. Scottdale, Penn.: Herald Press, 1985.

McCloud, Aminah Beverly. *African American Islam*. New York: Routledge, 1995.

Mintz, Jerome. *Hasidic People: A Place in the New World*. Cambridge: Harvard University Press, 1992.

Murphy, Joseph M. *Santeria*. Boston: Beacon Press, 1988.

Numbers, Ronald L. *Prophetess of Health: A Study of Ellen G. White*. New York: Harper & Row, 1976.

Numbers, Ronald L., and Jonathan M. Butler, eds. *The Disappointed: Millerism and Millenarianism in the Nineteenth Century*. Bloomington: Indiana University Press, 1987.

Palmer, Susan Jean. *Moon Sisters, Krishna Mother, Rajneesh Lovers: Women's Roles in New Religions*. Syracuse: Syracuse University Press, 1994.

Penton, M. James. *Apocalypse Delayed: The Story of the Jehovah's Witnesses*. Toronto: University of Toronto Press, 1985.

Sanders, Cheryl J. *Saints in Exile: The Holiness-Pentecostal Experience in African American Religion and Culture*. New York: Oxford University Press, 1996.

Sensbach, Jon F. *A Separate Canaan: The Making of an Afro-Moravian World in North Carolina, 1763–1840*. Chapel Hill: University of North Carolina Press,1998.

Shipps, Jan. *Mormonism: The Story of a New Religious Tradition*. Urbana: University of Illinois Press, 1985.

Sontag, Frederick. *Sun Myung Moon and the Unification Church*. Nashville: Abingdon Press, 1977.

Stein, Stephen J. *The Shaker Experience in America: A History of the United Society of Believers*. New Haven: Yale University Press, 1992.

Synan, Vicent. *The Holiness-Pentecostal Movement in America*. Grand Rapids: Eerdmans, 1971.

Tabor, James D. and Eugene V. Gallagher. *Why Waco?: Cults and the Battle for Religious Freedom in America*. Berkeley: University of California Press, 1995.

Thurman, Suzanne R. *O Sisters Ain't You Happy? Gender, Family, and Community among the Harvard and Shirley Shakers, 1781–1918*. Syracuse: Syracuse University Press, 2002.

Toews, Paul. *Mennonites in American Society, 1930–1970*. Scottdale, Penn.: Herald Press, 1996.

Turner, Richard Brent. *Islam in the African-American Experience*. Bloomington: Indiana University Press, 1997.

Vance, Laura L. *Seventh-day Adventism in Crisis: Gender and Sectarian Change in an Emerging Religion*. Urbana: University of Illinois Press, 1999.

Wacker, Grant. *Heaven Below: Early Pentecostals and American Culture*. Cambridge: Harvard University Press, 2001.

Watts, Jill. *God, Harlem U.S.A.: The Father Divine Story*. Berkeley: University of California Press, 1992.

Wessinger, Catherine. *How the Millennium Comes Violently: From Jonestown to Heaven's Gate*. New York: Seven Bridges Press, 2000.

Weisbrot, Robert. *Father Divine: The Utopian Evangelist of the Depression Era Who Became an American Legend*. Boston: Beacon Press, 1984.

Wilson, Laura. *Hutterites of Montana*. New Haven: Yale University Press, 2000.

Wright, Stuart A., ed. *Armageddon in Waco: Critical Perspectives on the Branch Davidian Conflict*. Chicago: University of Chicago Press, 1995.

Zborowski, Mark, and Elizabeth Herzog. *Life Is with People: Culture of the Shtetl*. New York: Schocken, 1962.

INDEX

ACKNOWLEDGMENTS

Thanks to my students at Indiana University, who have contributed to the development of my research agenda on alternative religions by stimulating and sharing my interest in outsider religious groups. Colleagues and administrators at Indiana University have consistently supported my endeavors. My wife Devonia, our children, and our granddaughter have created the circumstances that make such undertakings possible and pleasant.

TEXT CREDITS

p.13: *Records Kept by Order of the Church*, entry for Aug. 28, 1817. Manuscript at New York Public Library.

pp. 29–30: Robert Calef, *More Wonders of the Invisible World* (1700). Reprinted in George Lincoln Burr, ed., *Narratives of the Witchcraft Cases 1648–1706*. New York: Scribner's, 1914.

pp. 47–48: *Mennonite Year Book and Almanac for the Year of Our Lord 1913* p. 35.

pp. 66–68: *Testimonies of the Life, Character, Revelations and Doctrines of Our Ever Blessed Mother Ann Lee, and the Elders with Her; Through Whom the Word of Eternal Life Was Opened in This Day of Christ's Second Appearing: Collected from Living Witnesses, by Order of the Ministry, in Union with the Church.* Hancock, Mass.: J. Tallcott & J. Deming, 1816.

pp. 85–86: Charles Taze Russell, *"The Day of Vengeance": Millennial Dawn*, Vol. 4. Allegheny, Penn.: Watch Tower Bible and Tract Society, 1897.

pp. 102–04: Edwin S. Gaustad, ed., *A Documentary History of Religion in America to the Civil War*. Grand Rapids, Mich.: William B. Eerdmans, 1982.

p. 122: Robert Weisbrot, *Father Divine: The Utopian Evangelist of the Depression Era Who Became an American Legend.* Boston: Beacon, 1983.

pp. 142–43: Frederick Sontag, *Sun Myung Moon and the Unification Church*. Nashville, Abingdon, 1977.

ART CREDITS

Fig. 1: New York Public Library, Rare Books Division; Fig. 2: Indiana University Library; Fig. 3: Winterthur Museum; Fig. 4: Houghton Library, Harvard University; Fig. 5: Shaker Museum and Library, Old Chatham, NY; Fig. 6: Loma Linda University, California; Fig. 7: Loma Linda University Heritage Room; Fig. 8: Watchtower Bible and Tract Society of New York, Inc.; Fig. 9: Herald Examiner Collection/Los Angeles Public Library; Fig. 10: The First Church of Christ, Scientist; Fig. 11: Graham Carmichael; Fig. 12: Library of Congress; Fig. 13: National Archives (342-B-ND-022B-K-KE-73820).

ABOUT THE AUTHOR

Stephen J. Stein is Chancellor's Professor of Religious Studies and adjunct professor of American history at Indiana University, Bloomington. The focus of his research and teaching is American religious history, with special attention to eighteenth-century religious thought, outsider religious groups throughout American history, and topics relating to apocalyptic themes.

Stein is the author of *The Shaker Experience in America: A History of the United Society of Believers*, which received the American Society of Church History's Philip Schaff Prize. He is the editor of volume 3 in *The Encyclopedia of Apocalypticism* and volumes 5 and 15 of *The Works Of Jonathan Edwards*. He is currently working on an edition of Edwards's scriptural commentary known as the "Blank Bible." In 1994 Stein served as president of the American Society of Church History.